I Get It Now!

Jeanette Eichhorn

ISBN: 978-1734005509

Edited: Linda Hull
Author Photo: Makenna Oliver
Cover Design: Marianne Nowicki

Publishing Services rev. date: 11/17/2019

To:

I dedicate this book to my children, to which I know this is part of your story too. To all the children that have to develop their own structure in life. To my devoted and supporting husband and family. Thank you for forgiving me and supporting me through this journey.

Acknowledgements:

This book has definitely been a journey of pain, harsh realization, and will open all my strengths and weaknesses to the world. I am grateful for the experiences and opportunity to tell my story. In reading this I hope you Get it Now for yourself.

To my children, you have experienced most of this with me. I hope and wish that your journeys lead to a fulfilled life of joy.

To my mother, I know you were fighting your demons and your loss of joy. I love you and thank you for loving me.

To my former husbands, thank you for loving me and blessing me my beautiful children.

To my Family, there has always been love around me although I may not have seen it. Thank you for loving me.

To my Husband Scott, Words cannot express the love and forgiveness and the joy we share together. I love you.

The Aspen Tree:

An Aspen tree can live through a drought, a flood, it can be stepped on, and it can be cut in half. No matter the drama it receives the Aspen will always overcome defeat. It is because the seed it came from is one of the strongest in plant life. No matter how bad life is for that tree it will always flourish. The Aspen will start small and always grow, get better, and get more beautiful.

~ Francisco Valdez

Chapter 1

"I can't believe it's unlocked." I looked at my daughter as we pushed open the back door.

"Are we going to get in trouble for trespassing?" she asked before reluctantly following me into the dark and quiet building.

"Hope not." I ran my hand down the hallway wall where previous exotic dancers had once walk out to hustle money.

This isn't the normal place you'd bring your daughter to show her where you once worked. But she is quickly growing up and needs to hear the truth behind my story and where I came from, so she'll hopefully never have to walk in my shoes.

With the back door left open, light filtered down the hall and into the main room, a room I led my daughter into, holding her hand.

"You danced on that stage?" she asked. Even though the room was partially dark, the stage was extremely recognizable without the thick fog of cigarette smoke that once filled the room.

I dropped her hand and made my way onto the stage, glancing out to the room that was once packed with men looking for an escape from their daily lives and fantasized about the girl I once was. An empty feeling came over me, a feeling I wasn't expecting. I had worked my ass off to get into this strip club, I had worked my ass off while I was here, and I had worked my ass off to get out of here. The strange thing is that I missed it, and in the same thought I hated it.

I wish I had a silver spoon story to share with my kids, but it was just the opposite for me. Now I want to share my story with them, not for entertainment but to create a drive, a drive that will help make them successful.

I have spent the last fourteen years sheltering my children from my dark past. My youngest, who stands in the room with me, just recently learned that her two oldest siblings are from two different fathers.

"Show me some moves, Mom!" Ashton yelled in the room.

I ran my hand along the brass pole in the center of the stage, remembering the countless spins I made around it. It was almost like it was alive, but the pole never moved, it never spoke. Yet it consumed the souls of countless girls. Strange how being told you're beautiful and sexy from a stranger with a fistful of ten-dollar bills can suck the life from you.

"This is a place I prayed you'd stay far from."

"Kind of intriguing," she answered.

I stopped and looked at her.

"What? Mom! I'm not interested in becoming a stripper!"

Intriguing! The very word that I feared I would hear from her or my other daughter. Intriguing! The only word that could describe my first night on stage at a rundown, smoke-filled strip bar in Arkansas.

"You girls aren't supposed to be in here!" A deep voice echoed from the hall, scaring the living shit out of us. We both jumped like we'd been shot.

"I brought my daughter to show her where I once worked," I replied to the shadow.

He stepped into the light. "Why would you bring your daughter to an abandon strip club?"

"So she would know to never come back."

He paused for what seemed like an hour, then politely nodded his head. "Make sure that door locks behind when you leave." He turned and disappeared down the hall.

"Oh my gosh, Mom! That scared the crap out of me, can we go?"

I hopped down off the stage, then asked her to sit beside me. "I want you to know that life isn't going to be easy. And there are going to be many mountains and many valleys. What makes a person successful isn't how they climb the mountains; it's how they walk in the valleys."

She rolled her eyes. "Ok, Mom! Are you going all hippy on me?"

"Just entertain me for a moment. And I want you to hear me when I say this. The decisions I made in my life were out of necessity. I have worked very hard so that your decisions can be made from a place of choice. It's your choice and your decision whatever path you might take. My prayer for you is that you set your children up the same." I took a deep breath and fought off the tears. "I haven't set foot in this place for fourteen years. Because fourteen years ago, someone walked in here and gave me a choice."

Chapter 2

2424 Railroad Avenue in North Little Rock Arkansas—
my birth home. It's nothing to brag about, but it was home,
and I have many memories. The house was a long, white,
wood-sided duplex with a small front porch that faced a set of
railroad tracks. Hence the name, Railroad Avenue. I don't
really remember much about the neighborhood, but I do
remember the freight trains that barreled down the track at all
hours of the day and night, only seventy-five feet from my
bedroom. My imagination strikes with thoughts of items
falling off my dresser and picture frames crashing to the floor;
no matter how many times that would happen, my mother
would rehang them. But that's only my imagination, sparked
from movies about similar apartments set too close to railroad
tracks.

One picture I do remember hanging in my bedroom was
from my first birthday party, a party that my aunt hosted at her

house. Nobody remembers their first three or four birthdays, but there always seems to be a family member who could describe it in detail. For me, that person was my aunt Amada. Her memory carried a few descriptive scenes that I don't care to hang onto, but there's one that I have held close to the heart: the story of my dad.

My father was from Trujillo, Peru, and if you know anything about Peruvians, you know that the majority of them are dark-complexed and have exquisite skin. My father was one of those—his eyes were piercing, his olive skin was smooth and perfect, his build was masculine, and there is no question why my mother married him. My question would be why she couldn't stay married to him.

As a matter of fact, my mother missed my first birthday party because she was marrying my stepfather. I am not sure why she didn't wait, move the date of my birthday party, or just get married later in the day. Regardless of her decision, it started here—the abandonment, the emotional abuse, and the hell that my life turned into.

I was sitting in an old, decrepit hand-me-down highchair, devouring a piece of cheesecake layered in deep purple blueberries, wearing a blue flight suit. Not pink, like most mothers dressed their little girls in, but a little blue flight suit, because my father was very proud of becoming a supervisor at the Little Rock Airport.

Now, to paint a picture of this party, you have to understand that with my father's heritage came many Peruvian traditions. The cake was one of many. The home was decorated with bright colors and a rainbow of balloons and ribbons that seemed to be out of place in the small apartment. One tradition with Peruvians—they spare no expense when it comes to birthday parties.

My happy birthday song was sung in both English and Spanish, and looking back at pictures, I see myself leaning against my father in my flight suit, smiling from ear to ear. All the pictures I have come across from the past show a joyful and attentive man, someone who loved all and who was loved by all.

Mom? Well, Mom battled her demons throughout the years. Thin and petite, she had a model's body with flowing red hair that curled past her milky, fair, freckly skin. Looking through my grandmother's family album, I could see what my father had seen in her, a beautiful fireball with plenty of grit. But I do ask myself, only knowing my mother for the wreck that she is now after battling 27 years of drug abuse: How was she ever a girlfriend, a wife, a mother?

My stepfather, my mother, and I lived in the duplex for just over five years, and I remember Dad coming over many times, many times that I believed he was there to see me. But looking back, I now realize that he was there to see with my mother, his ex-wife. They would sit in the living room for hours talking about the good old times and looking back, I question why they ever split. But that is my imagination wanting normality in my family life. I know my mother wasn't easy to live with.

One day that I remember like it was yesterday was when Dad showed up with a present for me. A Ronald McDonald doll. Not Barbie, not Strawberry Shortcake, not even Ken, but a fuzzy redhead doll with thick white makeup that would scare the hell out of most five-year-old girls. Not me though, I loved it. McDonald's was a special memory for me; I still distantly remember making several trips with my father. He would always hold my hand walking in, point at the menu, and order the same thing every time. To this day, I will occasionally order my father's meal: a plain hamburger, fries, and a coke.

It was the summer of 1984 and the day that we said our goodbyes to the duplex that had been so good to us. There wasn't a dramatic ending where I watched the old, faded white house slowly disappear in the distance—it was just us driving off and heading north to the small Arkansas town of Vilonia.

My stepfather, Edward, was also a good man and had moved us into the country town on ten acres he had bought. It wasn't long before his parents bought the place next to us, giving me a place to run to when the shit hit the fan. A place that wasn't surrounded by traffic and liquor stores, just nature.

The town was small and country, the school was all-Caucasian, and there wasn't much for a six-year-old girl to do but catch bugs and play outside. Edward had created a family atmosphere to his best ability with an old, dilapidated single-wide trailer and what little money he made. The nights were quiet, with only Mother Nature making sounds outside, no trains, no sirens—it was something that I knew I could get used to, but my story isn't that easy, nor is it simple. Learning to beat adversity isn't easy, and to achieve that one has to be put through . . . well, just plain shit! It all started with a sit-down talk with Edward while my mother bawled her eyes out in the background.

Chapter 3

Seven years old: an age at which a little girl should never have to bury her father. I had experienced a lot by the time I was seven, but seeing cancer win against my father's life was a blow to me that took years to learn to live with. Many people, including family members, gave me advice that *in time it would pass and the emotions I was dealing with would disappear.* Bullshit! Losing my father at an early age was something I never got over. I learned to live with it, but I never got over it.

However, I was fortunate to have a great man who was there to soften the blow and create a strong male influence in my life. Edward wasn't nominated for the "father-of-the-year award," nor did he write a book on how to be the best dad. But he did the best he knew how in being my stepdad, and he delivered his care 100 percent, something for which I will always be grateful.

10

Being my first funeral, I was told it was like every other funeral. There was a wake, a service, then a burial. It took place in the small urban church where my father had met my mother. I remember the smell of old wood, the echo of every voice, and the floors creaking as I walked down the aisle. I froze at the fourth pew, staring at a dark wood-frame casket and the face of an unrecognizable man.

Cancer had stolen what little muscle mass he had, left him with a yellowish color that was painted in my memory, and some half-rated mortician had put a wig on him that didn't match anything about him. He looked horrible, and with a shaking hand, I reached in and touched the skin on the back of his hand. My whole life, my father was always reaching out for me, holding my hand, lifting me into the air, giving me hugs and sweet goodnight kisses, all warm touches. Now, he was just cold.

You also have to keep in mind that it was 1985, Michael Jackson had just come out with "Thriller," bright colors were in, and big hair was the thing. Along with mom jeans. And the 1980s showed up at my father's funeral. My father's entire family made the trip to the United States to bury him, a very large Hispanic family. I sat in the corner of the funeral home, listening to conversations in a foreign language while my mother remained an emotional wreck, confusing both my stepfather and stepmother about her true feelings for my father.

11

I thought back on my visits to his home and how clean he kept his house, how his family would sit at a table at night and eat the most amazing Peruvian meals, and sometimes all lie on an oversized couch and watch boxing while my father enjoyed a nice cold beer. My father ran his house as a normal family, something that was foreign to me since his life was cut so short.

Me? I just got stares from people I didn't know and conversations in Spanish, which I could only imagine involved pointing at me for being the dirty little country girl. My mother preached to me that dirty was bad. Shit, dirt in my life was good, or at least I thought so. I was able to come and go as I wanted, I played rough with the other kids that lived nearby, I fished for crawdads in the ditch, and I did many other kid things—dirt was part of my life. How could that be bad? But looking back and compared to the people in my father's family, yeah, I was the dirty kid. And damn proud of it!

I wasn't allowed to go to the burial, and it wasn't until my adult life that I learned where they had laid him to rest. After the funeral, I was sitting on the front porch of our trailer, dusting myself off from playing in a dirt pile, when a parade of cars pulled into our drive. The whole Peruvian family came to visit and spend time with me. Here I was, standing on a makeshift porch in front of our single-wide trailer, covered in dirt and matted hair, a complete embarrassment to my mother.

One by one, they spoke in broken English and Spanish to me, and I didn't have a clue what they were saying. They weren't really smiling just kind of patting my head and, I assume, saying sorry for my loss. My uncle stepped on the porch, and he was the spitting image of my father, it actually blocked my memories of the funeral. I ran and tried to jump in his arms. "Daddy, you're alive!" I thought that maybe all the talking in Spanish was explaining that my father was alive and here to see me.

My uncle pushed back. "Not Dad!" He pointed to himself. "Freddy." Everyone stood helpless on the porch until my mother snatched me up and sent me inside the trailer. I spent the rest of the day sitting in my room listening to my father's family, and at the end of their conversation, my mother walking them out. I didn't see them again until years later when I went to visit them.

Life kept moving, and with school not important to me or my mother, I found myself at the age of eleven making my own decision whether to go or not. I don't remember any of my teachers' names—I don't know if that is because they had no impact on my life or if I wasn't there enough to know who they were. But one name I do remember was Lynette.

Lynette was my dearest childhood friend. Her first name was Mellissa, but she went by her middle name, Lynette, because my name was Jeanette. She was tall, I was short. She had white, fair skin; I had my father's dark olive skin. She had

long, flowing blonde hair, and I had long, dark brown hair—
were we a pair! Lynette and Jeanette, riding three-wheelers,
playing outside, harassing every living creature in our little
world, and just being a couple of country girls. She lived just
about a mile or so away from my house. Her parents were
wonderful to me. Lynette was wonderful to me; I don't think
she ever recognized how socially different we were, the poor
trailer trash girl and the normal nuclear-family girl.

Imagine allowing children, girls at that, ages eight to ten,
to ride up and down the street on three-wheelers and be out all
day until darkness covered our little world, seems a bit insane
nowadays. But we had no worries, nor did our parents have
any concerns. I spent many days and nights under the safety of
Lynette's roof, enjoying a normal family environment. I don't
recall her ever staying at my house, and at the time I never
noticed.

*To all the friends in my life (many of whom are in this
book), let me stop and say thank you for your non-judgment
and love. Recognizing this much later in life was one of the
many reasons for me to write this book, and has shaped this
very strong, determined, and compassionate woman.*

Chapter 4

Although we had moved north of Little Rock, what seemed like a journey away for a child, my stepfather continued to work there. He spent hours every day on his commute with traffic and others from the small town that made the same fifty-to-sixty-mile trek. At that time, long-distance phone calls were very costly, and with only one income we lived poor, resulting in a lack of communication with my friends and family in North Little Rock. Early mornings and late-night arrivals left my mom very secluded and lonely. Long days of mundane tasks, with no money and no means of entertainment, left her with a desire for intimacy. This is what she found with our neighbor across the street.

I still remember the diluted gossip of family members suspicious of my mom's frequent trips down our long drive and across the road. Shit, she walked right in front of my grandparents' trailer. Did she know they knew? Did she care? Maybe she wanted to get caught. Well, she did.

One Saturday morning, my stepdad woke my stepsister and me up and we headed out to Conway Lake for some fishing. It is definitely a great memory, casting and catching and trying to outdo my stepsister and make Edward proud of me. My younger brother and my mom were sleeping in on that restful Saturday morning. We returned from fishing, and no one was home. My stepfather began calling family members to see if they had seen my mother. He reached my aunt, who said, "She dropped little John off several hours ago to run errands and go shopping."

Here we go...the first turbulent event of many to come.

Dad drove to my aunts to pick up my stepbrother. My brother had a tremendous speech impediment, so much that most people could not understand his words, but as soon as we picked him up, he uttered the sentence, "Mom's over at Dwight's." Clear as day!

Now, why would you get up, get the kid dressed, take him to your sister-in-law, then go back home (or next door) to sleep with a man? As a mother and a wife, I ask myself this question. Did she want to get caught? Did she think no one would figure it out? My stepdad drove like a bat out of hell heading home, turned on the TV, and told the three of us to sit on the couch and stay put. The sound of his heavy footsteps storming to his bedroom told us what was coming. He returned to the living room holding his 30/30 rifle, instructed us not to go outside no matter what we heard, and burst out the door.

Our trailer was set back from the road a couple hundred feet, but it wasn't far enough to keep us from hearing, "Edward, don't shoot him!" followed by screams, shouts, cuss words, flying pots and pans. The fight made it back to our drive where my mother started loading the car.

My stepdad yelled, "You are not taking the kids!"

Her reply was, "You can't keep Jeanette!" She loaded the car up with whatever she could grab, came into the house and snatched my arm hard enough to lift me off the ground and dragged me into the vehicle. I saw Edward crane over the car to see if the neighbor was still outside. I'm sure if he had been, Edward would've lowered the sights of the 30/30 on him and laid him down in his tracks. But the screaming from my mother brought his attention back to the car as we fishtailed out of the drive and headed to North Little Rock where her mother lived.

I left Vilonia, Arkansas that day, never getting to say goodbye to Lynette or explain what was happening and why I was leaving. I sat in the front seat watching the city limits of

Little Rock come into view and then the neighborhood of my grandmother's house.

At first, it seemed like the best situation for an eleven-year-old child to be at her happy place—Grandma's house! But that day proved quickly that this could not be anywhere close to a safe or a happy place. My mom dropped me off, and I remember that I was happy as pie. A lot of family lived at my grandmother's house: my mentally handicapped uncle, my two other uncles, my aunt, and her three kids, another aunt, and anyone else who needed somewhere to stay—my grandmother never turned anyone away. My grandmother fed me my favorite foods and put me to bed on the couch.

Things seemed great…but Mom had gone to get drunk or high or both. She ended up driving back to Vilonia to claim her stepchildren and violently kicked in the door—this is where the fight really began. She attacked my stepdad and he called in reinforcements—a few friends, his sister, and the entire church congregation.

My stepdad wasn't perfect and had his own demons he fought with, but he was faithful to his church, and not just any church, but a loud, bible-beating Pentecostal Church. Now, I am not sure where the Pentecostals stand with casting out real demons or if that is just a Catholic thing, but two-thirds of his church showed up at the house to pray over my mother. Yeah, not the best idea.

By now, Mom had fought hard enough to tire out, and with the alcohol and drugs in her system, she sat on the couch, adamant that she was taking the kids. I'm not sure if she heard the commotion outside, but Edward opened the front door and let in everyone who could fit in the room. Mom was sitting on the couch, clueless to what was going on, but once their leader, maybe the pastor, started talking, so did Mom. The words I was told she used were, "Fuck y'all!" Several times.

I don't think this church knew what they were getting themselves into, but this is where Mom began the first of many attempts to kill herself, cutting her wrist and bleeding all over the couch and floor, and part of the congregation.

At my grandmother's house, we were awakened at 2 a.m. by a phone call. My stepdad instructed my grandmother that she needed to come get her crazy daughter. When we arrived, they were loading her into an ambulance. She was strapped to the stretcher with bandaged arms and heavily sedated. We followed the ambulance to the hospital, where we were met by the police and a social worker who pulled me off to the side.

Now let me remind you that I was eleven years old. I had just witnessed an already stressful day turn into one of the most traumatic days of my life. Now the social worker asked me to decide who I wanted to live with, my grandma (my favorite person) or my stepdad (home). I remember making that decision, a decision that would haunt and shape my life completely. Why was it up to an eleven-year-old? Shouldn't it have been the most logical choice to keep me with my sister, brother, and father? I chose my grandmother because at the time I was scared of my mom going crazy again if I was at my dad's. I didn't think it was a permanent decision. Maybe more like a weekend visit.

Chapter 5

As the fall of 1988 rolled around so did the beginning of my teenage years. Mom had been out of the mental hospital for a few weeks, and we had moved from the small town of Vilonia back to the city of North Little Rock. Since my father's death, I had received $350 a month in his social security, definitely enough money for a young person to live happily on. Nope! My mother had taken every check for the last couple of years, and I never saw a dime.

The streets of my grandmother's neighborhood were broken asphalt and rocks, not an easy walk to the bus, much less around the block. Many retirees lived in the area, with the cost of living so cheap and the houses small and livable at best. The street we lived on was the dividing line for two high schools, one of them primarily African American and the other primarily redneck. Totally opposite.

We lived in a one-thousand-square-foot single house with three different families that totaled twelve people and only three bedrooms. Well, almost three bedrooms. My bed was the recliner in the living room, and my things were stored in my grandmother's room, stacked on top of each other. Not the greatest accommodations for a girl who was just coming into her own.

But that was my grandmother—no matter what my family did, she never threw anyone out of the house. I loved my grandmother, but as you can tell through my language, I felt she should have kicked all of them out except my mentally challenged uncle.

The first day of the school year came along with the excitement of returning to class but the idea of getting some normality in my life was quickly killed by the comment of a little girl sitting behind me. With a hand in the air, she called out to the teacher, "Jeanette has white things in her hair." I remember the incident like it was yesterday. The teacher asked me to go to the office with a note she had written, and after one look from the secretary, she announced to me and everyone else that I had head lice. I don't remember if I went home or they secluded me, but I do remember the embarrassment, horrible embarrassment that a seventh-grade girl could only have nightmares about.

There I was, on my first day of middle school with old ratty clothes and a severe case of head lice. "If I could only get the money from Mom, then I could buy clothes and shampoo," I said out loud back at Grandma's house. But wouldn't you know, one of my uncles overheard me and gave me his paycheck. I thanked him and snatched it up like a starving child—I kind of was.

I walked to the store a mile away and bought enough shampoo to last a month and a few pieces of clothing that I could switch out during the week. But with an overpopulated house of people, some of whom I wasn't even sure who they were, things came up missing. My shampoo and clothes were some of many things I lost over my time at my grandmother's. I had bought a cute little blouse that came up missing, but I found it when my mother walked in one day having cut out the sleeves. The rage that flowed through my veins fueled me for a fight I had been contemplating for a year. That was the first night the police came for a visit. After that, they came often.

One place I could get away from everyone and everything that haunted my life was the roof of my grandmother's house. Many nights I would climb the tree just outside the back door to my solitude area, a place I would try to count the stars and dream of walking on the moon. As cold weather moved into the area the time spent in my solitude area was cut short. With cold weather came the holidays.

Christmas is a time of joy and excitement for people of all ages, but not for families of low incomes. That Christmas, my grandmother managed to buy me two presents with her social security money and hid them in the house—I know this because she told me later in life. Christmas Eve, from my spot on the recliner, I watched my aunt and uncle sneak into the living room and set up Christmas for my cousins. I watched them unpack gift after gift from three bags and place them under "their" tree. I couldn't help it—I burned with jealousy and envy. I wanted their gifts so badly that it turned my stomach. The following morning, I watched my cousins unwrap gift after gift, thank their parents, and then throw each one into a pile with the others.

My grandmother went to get my two presents, and it turned out my other uncle and aunt had taken them. But my grandmother, the hero she is, gave me a couple of gifts that she had bought. And of course, the aunt and uncle with the huge Christmas were upset that she didn't buy them more than the one gift she bought all her grandchildren. Just plain bullshit selfishness. God, I hated them.

The summers were hot and somewhat isolated. Not much entertainment happened in the neighborhood, though a few times during my early teens I was able to go to Texas and stay with my father's family. Each year, it was three weeks I looked forward to—normal family life, food, and sleeping in a bed with sheets and a pillow.

Needless to say, we didn't live in the safest neighborhood in North Little Rock either; the want-to-be-Bloods-or-Crips lived throughout the area. The nights were often filled with the hollow echoes of sirens throughout the streets and the flashing lights of cop cars glaring into the windows in my grandmother's house. The school bus picked up and dropped off the kids one block east of my grandmother's, and many mornings a sweet neighbor would walk me to the bus stop to keep me safe.

One afternoon, the bus let me and a couple of kids off in the normal spot, and I wasn't three steps into my walk home when I heard someone behind me. "Hey, little white girl!" a young black guy wearing his red gang colors yelled at me. It wasn't him talking to me that scared me, it was the fact that he and two others were following me and quickly gaining. I had heard the stories of girls being raped in the neighborhood, and there was no doubt it was my turn. I ran like hell.

I'm not sure why I didn't run straight to my grandmother's house—a little scared of letting them know where I lived? I ducked down an alley and sprinted the length of it before my ankle twisted on a rock and sent my body crashing to the pavement. I felt a sharp pain radiate down my arm and caught a glimpse of blood as I climbed back to my feet and continued to run. Thank God, I was fast. I lost them and made it safely to my grandmother's. I bandaged my arm and sat in the living room, shaking and panting.

The year my husband (he is a dentist) and I started dating he cut out a marble-sized piece of beer-bottle glass from my arm. Yep, it stayed embedded in my arm for fourteen years. His hygienist couldn't believe it. For me? It was just another scar.

Chapter 6

My grandmother was a hero in many ways. I don't mean to repeat myself, but she truly was, and during my transition from middle school to high school she was able to divert my father's checks to me. Finally, after all those years, I was able to buy much-needed shampoo and clothes to somewhat fit in with my classmates.

I never thought of myself as athletic and was certainly never told I was, but to pass the time, I tried out for volleyball my eight-grade year. And believe it or not, I made it and I was really good. I don't remember the coach's name, but at the beginning, she was really encouraging, and that was something that was extremely foreign to me. I then tried out for the basketball team and made it as well. Tried out for the softball team, made it. My life started to seem like an actual life.

The difference between sports and the classroom for me was that I excelled in sports and bombed in the classroom. The coaches loved me, and the teachers had different thoughts. The kids were also different—on the court and on the field I was treated as an equal, and in the classroom, I was picked on for being stupid or different. Sports shaped me into the businesswoman I am today, and I do my best to treat my employees like my coaches treated me. The old saying, "A kid never remembers what their teacher said but remembers everything their coach said," is so true.

But unfortunately, all good things can come crashing down, and because I didn't have gas money for my aunt to drive me around, I couldn't make all the games, which forced the coaches to let me go. And because my mother wouldn't help me and was more interested in her boyfriends, I became more and more hateful toward her. Occasionally she would take me to stay with her which meant sleeping in a run-down unfurnished apartment or in her car parked in a park. I don't really remember how she ended up winning the fight from my grandmother to drag me into her world or how many times it happened. This was definitely not a path for educational success. The late nights, the drugs, the drama she started—it all came to a boiling point.

Leaving Little Rock, the school, and my mother became my top priority but leaving my virginity behind was more a rebellious circumstance than the romance with a knight in shining armor I had imagined as a young girl. I remember like it was yesterday: One of my cousins and I went to a water park on a hot summer day. Towels wrapped around our shoulders, wearing sunglasses and flip flops, we were bad-asses. We entered the pool like we owned the place, gaining the attention of everyone. We swam for a short time, long enough to beat off the summer heat, and then found a couple of poolside chairs, where we flipped our wet hair over the ends of the headrests and soaked up some much-needed sun. It was possible that move attracted a couple of guys who made their way over to us. One of them was super cute and I had no problem talking with him. "It's hot out here, you want to get in the water?" He lured me in with no resistance.

We swam for a total of maybe sixty seconds, then locked up arm-in-arm and started making out. I'm not sure why the adults didn't break us up, or maybe they tried, but the kissing led to something else…me losing my virginity. Unbeknownst to the people lounging poolside and the other people swimming in the pool, I was sitting on this guy's lap and there was much more going on that they couldn't have imagined. It hurt like a son-of-a-bitch!

I was never taught by anyone the importance of safe sex, or for that matter, how to even have sex. I do remember the girls in the locker room talking about how the first time, aka popping the cherry, would cause bleeding. *Holy Shit! What if I bleed in the pool? Everyone will know.* I was so relieved when he was done and nothing was seen, but I can honestly say that all I got from the experience was pain that lasted close to a week. Something I have always regretted but I am sure 95%

of the women today would agree with me on losing their virginity.

I loved my grandmother, but I felt that my time was up in Little Rock, so I packed what little I had and moved to Vilonia with my other set of grandparents on my stepfather's side. They lived in a dirty, rundown, single-wide trailer with a porch that had fallen in and a driveway that wasn't passible during rain. They were sweet people, kind of, but they also knew I received $350 a month. There were little hints from them that I should give them the money, but I made it clear that I was holding on to it. "That's fair. But you'll have to pay rent," they responded. So, at age fourteen, I paid rent to live with my grandparents.

Over time, word got out to the rest of the family in Vilonia that I was paying rent, and my cousin and her mother begged me to move in with them. Her mother was known as a person that was always trying to get rich quick, and my first thought was, *everyone wants my money*! But that wasn't the case here—in fact, the money was never brought up, nor any guidance or rules.

Upon moving back to Vilonia, considering I didn't have any grades from North Little Rock, I was forced to repeat the ninth grade. I was pissed at first, but since I didn't have anyone pushing me to go to school, I hardly ever went. My cousin was a sweet and popular girl with very little parental guidance, and together we managed to stay out many nights and were constantly enjoying our teenage years.

We both landed jobs at Shoney's—I was a hostess and Michele was a waitress. We worked nights and weekends when we weren't in school, and even worked when we were supposed to be in school. The restaurant was forty-five minutes away and the late nights and many drives we shared only drew us closer. One of our favorite things to do after work was to go and cruise Conway, Arkansas. I know many of you might not understand the term "cruise," but being in the car with your best friend and having nowhere to go was what was so special about that time.

A year passed by, and things were great at my cousin's house until the night her little sister and I had a blowout fight. She was a couple of years younger than I, so we had developed a sister relationship. Our fight was simple—I disagreed with her lifestyle, and she didn't like me sharing my advice. Sister stuff. But the fight was bad enough that I packed my things and left that night. Michele wasn't even at home at the time and didn't learn until the next day that I had moved out.

There isn't a day that goes by I don't think about Michele and the fun and crazy times we shared. So, again, I left Vilonia in my wake and headed back to North Little Rock and to a life that wasn't healthy.

I moved in with my aunt, two cousins on my mother's side, my aunt's boyfriend, and two other people with a baby. Of course, this was all in another single-wide. I had blossomed into an attractive, dark-haired teenager and was known in the family as the "pretty one." This was good and bad. Good for my self-esteem, bad for attracting the men in the family and pulling out the demonic jealousy in my cousins. I'm still pissed about one of my cousins ruining my stereo by throwing milk on it during a shouting fight, all over her mother allowing me to drive the car to see my friends.

I had continued to work at Shoney's, saving my monthly checks and occasionally going to school. I did my best to keep to myself in a love-hate relationship with anyone that came into my life. I was sixteen years old and, through learned behavior, managed to budget my money and become responsible. Needing transportation, I purchased a hot pink Honda Elite 50CC Moped. It only went thirty-five miles per hour, but I rode it on every road, street, and highway, pissing everyone off that was stuck behind me. Honking and giving me the middle finger was a regular occurrence that I only laughed at and looking back it was a "Dumb and Dumber" moment in my life. Of course, I had a little fun with it—the wooden bridge that served as my ramp still stands today.

But with cold weather and rain, a Moped wasn't the smartest choice of transportation, so with my earnings, I sold it and bought a car. A Honda CRV. What the dealer didn't explain to me was how expensive insurance was for a sixteen-year-old girl living on her own. I couldn't afford it, but all of my family begged me to keep it and just not have insurance; none of them did on any of their cars. But I knew the law, and at the age of sixteen, I took the car back to the dealership and told them I couldn't afford it, leaving me back where I started…on foot.

Chapter 7

The start of my junior year was a year of high hopes and strong intentions. I had just settled into my classroom desk when a voice came over the intercom asking for me to report to the counselor's office. *Great! What in the hell does the counselor want now? Is she sending me to another school? Is she making me start the tenth grade again? Or was my mom found dead from a drug overdose?* The thoughts raced through my mind as I made my way through the empty hallways. "Take a seat," the secretary replied without making eye contact. *Great, everyone knows the news but me.* I had planned to start the year out by flying under the radar, staying quiet, and keeping to myself. Not easy when you live with fifteen people in 1,000 square feet.

"Youth Challenge? Military? You have to be crazy," I told my counselor after she had explained there was no way in hell I would graduate and suggested I go to a program designed for high school students in "my circumstance."

I didn't have any choice—either go to Youth Challenge or figure something else out other than school. I snatched the flyer out of her hand and stormed out of the office, pissed as shit that she didn't give me any other choices. I stormed out the doors and into the school parking lot, not stopped by any teacher or coach, and sat down on a curb and looked down at the flyer. It read, "To Intervene and Reclaim the Lives of Teenagers." *Do I need to be reclaimed?* But I read more, and the further I read, the more interesting it became.

It wasn't for those looking for a second chance, or to become better citizens, but rather for kids who didn't have any other opportunities but still had the drive to make something for themselves. It was a place that gave kids time to focus on themselves, not in a selfish way but in a way to build character. It was as if the flyer was talking directly to me—this program was what I wanted. Leaving school, I went to my aunt's house and showed her the flyer, asking her if she would take me. "Whatever," she replied handing the flyer back to me. Then looking up at the desperation of getting out of here and making something of my life she agreed to take me.

The following day, I rode in the back seat staring out the window, trying my best to ignore the lingering eyes of my uncle glaring at me through the rearview mirror. Once we arrived at Youth Challenge, we made our way to the administrative building. The facility was located on a military base in Little Rock, and the buildings were basic and without any color or character, kind of cold. During registration, I got the impression they didn't care who was signing me in, just as long as they were family. My aunt and uncle waved their goodbyes to me at a distance while a tall man in a starched uniform pushed me into a line of unconventional teenagers. To this day, I am not sure if he saw the coldness of my family waving goodbye or was ready for his next class to start.

I definitely missed the part in the flyer that said it would be like basic training for the marine corp. The yelling started immediately. And I fell in love with it! Many of the other kids didn't, and since we were there voluntarily, many of them quit the first couple of days. Me? I thrived on the orderliness and neatness and stayed hyper-focused on the physicality of the requirements placed on a bunch of misfits like myself.

Many of the other kids spoke out, fought back, and were just plain assholes. I wanted to be known as one of the good kids and kept a low profile and did what I was asked. Other cadets became shadows in the malignant world in which I was finding myself. I didn't care to fit in. I just wanted to finish my five-and-a-half months, get my GED, and join my new love, the military.

I don't remember most of the other cadets' names, but I do remember Bo. He was a character, funny with loveable big brother traits. He always lightened the tension between cadets, made boring classes fun, and at every march came up with funny cadences. I laughed more at Youth Challenge with Bo than I had my life entire life.

Many of the cadets had communication with their families, but there were a select few that no one wrote or called, and I was part of that group. I was perfectly fine with that until visitor day, when my aunt and uncle showed up with news about my mother.

They actually had to tell me about this years later, because I don't remember them coming to let me know that my mother wasn't doing well. I do remember getting a pass to go home and see my family. It's funny how the little decisions we make have such huge consequences in our lives.

I went home, and within five minutes realized I didn't want to be there with those groping, pot-smoking, just plain white-trash people. Plus, my mother was fine, she was just being my mother.

My cousin asked if I would like to join her and her boyfriend on a camping trip to Lake Hamilton. *And not stay here during my pass? Hell yeah!* So, we drove an hour west and met one of their friends, a thirty-six-year-old single man who had his own boat and camper. We water skied throughout the day and enjoyed being lake bums, something I thoroughly loved. That evening, by the campfire, we sat around eating hotdogs, chips, and anything else that was in the camper. Then, out of the blue, my cousin brought out a couple of joints of weed. I had managed to make it sixteen years without smoking pot, but since it was just us, I figured what could it hurt? I never expected my cousin and her boyfriend to get so stoned that it would take me out of a safe environment.

A thirty-six-year-old man has a way with words for a sixteen-year-old girl. Being molested so many times throughout my childhood warped my perceptions of sex, and a grown man with gentle hands was something new. My fear wasn't that I had sex with him that night or that anyone would find out; come on, the consensual age for sex in Arkansas is sixteen. My fear was that I smoked weed, and if I was drug-tested at Youth Challenge I would be kicked out. How could I have let this happen?

With less than two months left in the program, I dropped out for fear of testing positive for marijuana. *So stupid!* Why don't we think about the consequences before we do dumb shit? Maybe because I was sixteen? Maybe because I wanted to fit in? Maybe because I was scared of saying no?

Anyway, now I was pregnant.

Recently, I spoke at a Youth Challenge facility with girls who were early in the program. They couldn't believe I had sat in the very chair they sat in, nor could they believe that I was from the second class to have ever gone through the program.

I found it rather amusing when one of the girls asked me if I'd ever gotten any visitors or if I was "that" girl.

I thought for a moment, sitting in an old wooden chair. "I was that girl," I answered. "My dad died when I was seven, and my mother was strung out somewhere in the city, I think." The little girl tried to change her question, but I wouldn't let her. "This is your time, your time for five months to work on yourself. There is no one here to please or impress, so focus on making you a better you."

I wished them luck and promised that I would return with a college recruiter to answer any questions they may have about going to college. Over the next few weeks, four of the girls wrote me letters thanking me for coming to talk, and their sweet words reminded me of how little we had while in the program.

Two-and-a-half months later, I walked in the door to a swarm of smiles and miles of hugs. Their self-confidence had returned, their physical appearance was strong, and their words broke my heart. "You actually came back?" most of them asked. These girls aren't guaranteed the many promises that are given to them, that they wish for. And for me to return with the college recruiter I had told them about was a big deal to them. Kept promises!

Chapter 8

Well shit, I guessed it was time to grow up, and at the grand old age of sixteen. I never did return to Youth Challenge in fear I would fail a drug test, and once you tested positive, you were out. I couldn't handle failure. Of course, it was a month after I had sex with the thirty-six-year-old that I found out I was pregnant. And of course, once I told him, he disappeared like he was being hunted by the mafia, and honestly, the mafia might have been gentler compared to the wrath of my crazy family.

My aunt's house wasn't ideal for a pregnant teenager. I didn't even have a room there, so I found my mother, who was living in government housing and crawled in with her. The news of me being pregnant elated her, and not because she was going to be a grandmother or because I had finally screwed up my life, it was so the focus wouldn't be on her for a change.

Shoney's gave me my old job back and actually moved me up to waitressing, where I could make more money. But with just one car between my mother and myself, there were times I couldn't get there. To help ends meet, I got another job as a cashier at a grocery store two blocks down from our government house.

I remember one night lying in bed and shivering under the covers because I was too lazy to climb out of bed and close the window. Just staring at the ceiling with lights flashing through the room from traffic outside, lost in deep thought. "I am sixteen and have pissed away most of my life, or maybe I was never given any life?" I mumbled feeling sorry for myself. "If there is a God up there, give me some sign that things are going to be better in my life." And I believe it was during that talk that my sign showed up. I hauled ass to the bathroom holding back what was coming up.

I threw up from the early part of my pregnancy to the very end. I mean, I was sick. I made several trips to the doctor to get different medications, but nothing helped. The doctor even preached to me about being bulimic.

"Bulimic? Shit, I just wish I could keep a fucking hamburger down." I eyed him.

"Maybe you should cut out the fast food and have a healthier choice of food," he replied.

Damn good thing my mother was strong, because this 125-pound, pregnant teenager was about to beat the living hell out of a doctor who quickly scurried out the door.

But in his defense, I was losing weight, and I mean losing it fast. I went from 125 to 95 over my pregnancy, and I ate everything I could get my hands on; I just couldn't keep it down.

I recall a time when I had fueled up our car and walked into the station to pay, and I lost it in the doorway. No one in and no one out thanks to this projectile vomiting, brown-haired girl, soon to be a mom. There are some other stories, but I'll save you the details and leave it to your imagination. Pregnancy sucks!

While working at the grocery store, I was checking out an elderly couple that had managed to buy just enough food for what they could afford when *he* walked by. I'm not sure if it was a hormonal pregnancy thing or just my natural teenager vibes, but Rob was freaking cute. He had worked at the grocery store longer than I had, but he'd been off the last month, and with his return to work, I was able to grow a smile. Ok, maybe he was twenty-two, but my baby daddy was thirty-six, so this was a good change.

We hung out maybe a week before we started officially dating—for some reason, it was important to him that everyone knew we were now an item. I didn't care who knew; this was the first person in my life who actually cared about me and a baby that wasn't even his. That spoke of chivalry to me. Rob wasn't that. I didn't find out until later in life.

It was during the month we dated that I learned Rob was heading to prison for burning down a federal building. He explained that if he was to marry, the court would give leniency and cut his time from a couple of years to just five months. So, we got married. And then he went to prison.

I drove three hundred miles every week to the prison, alone, pregnant, at the age of seventeen. Thinking back, I can't believe I was driving across the state. Today I won't let my daughter drive thirty miles to see her friends. It was insane how independent I was at such a young age and how I was able to raise an infant, work, and still put back money. I do believe it was the crazy times like these that shaped much of my life.

I had Dustin while Rob was in prison. My mother helped me the best she could, and I was able to take off work for a few weeks to recover from birth. Nothing made sense about this situation, but hey, during this time there wasn't anything to make sense out of. Plus, life goes on. Once Rob served his time, we had just enough money to move into a rental house and start our "wonderful" lives.

It is astonishing looking back at how supportive my family was for a pregnant teenager to marry a 23-year-old convicted felon. I was trusting a drug addict to help with my child and marrying an older man who was on his way to the big house. A world that looks completely upside down but to a sixteen-year-old it appeared normal.

Chapter 9

I now understand life after prison and the hardship ex-inmates go through trying to adapt. Society has painted "normal life" as this beautiful Norman Rockwell picture. If you know anything about people who have served time you know that they can't keep a job. Rob struggled over the following years, jumping from one job to another, and I felt sorry for him. He would lie about doing time just so he could get a job, and then one way or another his bosses would find out and fire him.

To help pay the bills, I got another job at Hardees, and for two years I worked three jobs and came home every night trying to be a wife and mother at the grand old age of eighteen. Our marriage wasn't horrible, just turbulent at times, but I wasn't wise enough to know that I was doing all the work. Everything we bought, rented, and borrowed was in my name; Rob didn't have any credit or a very good reputation for finances of any sort.

I, on the other hand, became savvy with money and even built a savings account. It definitely wasn't something I was taught or something I had read anywhere, I just had the natural gene for managing money, my money.

One Sunday evening, I was tending to my tables at Shoney's, refilling empty coffee cups and putting up with the rude church people, when I overheard one of my customers talking about real estate. "I only wish I could buy a house," I replied, pouring her a cup of coffee.

She eyed me through the steam rising from the porcelain cup. "Why wish?"

"Because I'm only eighteen years old and work three jobs to make ends meet on rent."

"Anyone can buy a house." She slid one of the chairs back from the table and nodded for me to sit. I did. Over the next hour of listening to her, and helping my tables, I learned about putting money down and what I could afford.

"You got to be shitting me!" I exclaimed, looking at the figure she wrote down on the back of a napkin on what I could afford.

She smiled really big. "I don't shit anyone." She picked up pretty quickly that I was rough around the edges and carried the language of a sailor.

I went home and shared the conversation with Rob, who was engrossed in a TV show and pretty much blew me off. But it didn't matter, after hearing the lady talk about owning a piece of property and becoming part of the American dream, I was hooked on working harder.

It's funny the people who cross your path and change your life with just some words. I really wish I would have gotten that lady's name to be able to thank her for starting to make my dreams come true.

During the fall of 1996, I purchased our first home for $27,000 in Jacksonville, Arkansas, a small community north of Little Rock. The small craftsman-style house had belonged to an elderly woman who could no longer live on her own. The side of the house had been turned into a beautiful courtyard covered in wisteria and lined with cobblestones that encompassed a water fountain. The respect for keeping this yard in shape gave me the green thumb I now have, and my love for plants. My front yard was fenced off from the neighborhood and everything dwarfed a gargantuan magnolia tree that rose from the center of the yard. I can still smell the flowers that bloomed every spring and brought a warmth of peace when I would sit outside, staring at the plants that I helped keep alive. It was heaven! My home. What else could a girl ask for?

And like all young married couples, we settled into our home with our little family...and nine months later, a baby girl named Amber.

At this time, I was loving life even though my schedule was crazy. Up at 4 a.m., take Dustin and Amber to Grandmother's house, work three jobs, and then back home at 9p.m. five days a week and half days on the weekend. Rob was in and out of work, and I can remember the conversation like it was yesterday. We were sitting in the living room with the kids in bed, talking about how in the hell we could get caught up and make more money. "My buddy's girlfriend is a dancer at a club in Little Rock," Rob said, looking at a blank TV.

"Fuck that shit! I am not taking my clothes off for no amount of money."

"He said she clears $600 a night."

I didn't answer—maybe there was an amount of money.

The truth of the story was that Rob went to this particular club on occasions with his friends, and since I was only nineteen years old, I couldn't get in. There were a few times I went and tried to get in—I didn't want Rob in the club with some strange girl grinding all over him, but the owner would turn me away at the door.

"Sorry, honey. Gotta be twenty-one to get in the club. Unless you want to work for me?" she said every time. Tell me Arkansas isn't messed up on some laws—you have to be twenty-one to get into a strip club, but you only have to be eighteen to be on stage taking off all your clothes.

One evening, after being turned away at the door, we came back home to a kitchen table stacked with bills—a depressing sight when you first walk in. We sat on the couch and talked about me dancing. $600 dollars a night was a hell of a lot of money for us. We figured if I would dance just a couple of times, it would help us catch up.

Chapter 10

The sun had begun its trek toward the horizon, casting an orange fire within the clouds. I stood behind my car, staring at what looked like a painting. Then I turned and faced the door that led into the club where I was going to start my dancing career. *What in the fuck am I doing?* was the thought that played over and over in my head. I opened the door, casting a ray of bleeding sunshine into the club. The dust particles in the air filled the doorway, and I felt like I wasn't any bigger than one of those specks.

I know it was my imagination, but when the door shut, it sounded like wrought-iron gates slamming closed. I was greeted by the lady who owned the place, the same lady who wouldn't let me in the door as a customer. With a cold arm around my shoulder and a Virginia Slim hanging out of her mouth, she led me back to the dressing room and to the other girls. I was welcomed with a strangely warm vibe, something you wouldn't expect from a group of girls whom I had labeled as sluts and whores.

"Thank God we have some new blood. I won't have to dance as much tonight," one of the girls replied.

"I thought the more you danced the more money you made," I answered.

Another girl walked up to me. "Not everyone wants to work." She held out her hand and introduced herself to me.

Arkansas only allowed topless dancing with no lap dances—a three-foot law was what they called it. The only way girls were to make money was on stage, dancing. Yeah, that law was made to be broken. Behind closed doors, all dancers gave lap dances and that three-foot law disappeared much like the self-dignity of the dancers. What I didn't understand was why a few of the girls were in the business but didn't want to dance as much as they could. Me, I was here for the money and I planned to work my ass off.

I learned through the years of dancing at other clubs that if a new girl came in and made more money than the veterans, she was going to get her ass kicked. Not at this club. I also learned that if you hustled another girl's customer, you'd get your ass kicked. Not at this club.

The first time on stage I was every bit a fish out of water. I was athletic and had no dance skills, but I also had something called stage fright. With the music blaring in the background, my mind flowed with the beat like clouds flowing with the wind. My body? Shit, I have no idea what the hell it was doing.

A couple of men approached the stage and held up a couple of five-dollar bills, so I must have been doing something right . . . *or were they making fun of me . . . or did they feel sorry for me?* Then it hit me: *Just take the damn money.* I did, and it's funny how sliding money out of the hand of customers can build self-confidence and self-esteem.

The money kept coming and so did my moves, and before long I was into a groove. And just like Rob's friend, I made over $600 the first night.

And in the mix of all this Rob had decided to go to trucking school. He landed a contract with a company that agreed to pay for his school if he worked for two years with them. I resumed my three jobs while he attended school and when he finished, I was able to take a deep breath and cut back on one of my jobs. Right? He quit work within the first year and we acquired his debt of school.

Now with more debt and larger bills working three jobs wasn't getting us anywhere. So, my bright idea was to move in with my grandmother and rent out our house. I had heard that rental property was a great income, and what could possibly be wrong with moving two small kids and an out-of-work husband in with family?

By this time, the only people left at my grandmother's house were my mentally handicapped uncle and another uncle that had as much trouble keeping a job as Rob. We took the front bedroom as ours, a room that measured 10x10 feet, and moved in what belongings we could along with Dustin and Amber.

Rob was a bit of a charmer — sometimes a little too well, and my grandmother would listen to his bullshit, though she thankfully never fully bought it. I continued to wear myself down working three jobs and dancing on the side and Rob and I started fighting—and I mean fighting.

On a few occasions, my grandmother would ask us to take it outside or she'd call the police. She had a fear that our fights would escalate into some pretty rough altercations, like those that my other family was known for. But we kept our hands down and only fought with our words. I often wondered if fist fighting would have been less painful.

Our problems finally grew to renters not paying, Rob not working, me working myself down, and everything else associated with money. I had married at sixteen, gotten pregnant, and didn't have a clue about marriage, husbands, or being a wife. But by twenty, I thought I had figured out what a husband should be, and Rob wasn't it.

I came in late from a shift at work and was greeted by my kids at the door wanting supper. I looked at Rob on the couch. "It's 9:30. You haven't fed the kids?"

"I think your grandmother might have given them something," he replied, never taking his eyes off the TV.

"You don't work! You can at least feed the kids and not make my grandmother do it."

"She likes to," he replied, not really hearing what I had said.

I calmly walked the kids into the kitchen and fixed them mac and cheese, then went back into the living room. I was tired of fighting, tired of pulling all of the weight, and just plain tired.

"I want you out of here and I want a divorce." That, he heard.

"Shut up and go eat with the kids!"

"Get your fucking ass up and out of here!" I stood my ground.

The yelling started, first with name-calling, but what I didn't expect or see coming was the lamp Rob grabbed and hurled in my direction. The crashing explosion of the lamp shattering against the wall caused everyone in the house to come into the living room.

My grandmother shouted, "Alright you two! I called the police."

We continued to yell at each other, only sub-consciously hearing what my grandmother had said, and once the police arrived, it settled down with the instructions from the police. Plus Rob, being a felony, knew not to push in front of the police.

Rob pointed his finger to me and his statement of it "not being over" sent me over the edge. I should have been a responsible twenty-year-old mother and collected my thoughts, but at twenty I went back into the house and called a friend of mine who lived in California.

"Angel? I need to get the fuck out of here. Could I come to stay with you and your husband for a short time?"

"You need a fresh start, come on," she pleaded.

Angel, and her husband Robby, had friended me while Rob was in prison. They were in the military and had recently moved to California. Our conversations on the phone had painted a beautiful picture of Sacramento and I couldn't think of a better place to go. With my grandmother begging me to stay, no cell phone, and two hundred dollars to my name, I left Little Rock with my two small kids and headed west.

Chapter 11

The lights from the oncoming traffic blurred my vision through the tears that continued to fall to the floorboard of my car. Tears made of hatred, emotional turmoil, and fear of the unknown. The first two hundred miles, I couldn't answer Dustin as to why we were leaving and how long we would be gone. "Just try and get some sleep," I coached him, praying that I could have this time to myself and figure out what I was going to do.

I had made long trips in the past but nothing over eleven or twelve hours—this trip would easily double that distance. Oklahoma seemed to never end. I wasn't sure if it was because of the length of the drive or that my blood was still boiling. But after some time, I began to cool down and started answering Dustin's question as best I knew how. They were questions that I was asking myself as well.

As each semi-truck passed going in the opposite direction, I wondered if they had been in California. The wind that drafted behind them shook my little car and reminded me just how small I really was. I was focused on making it to Sacramento without stopping for the night, mainly because of the lack of funds, and to my surprise, it was easier than I expected.

Throughout the night, my thoughts drifted from my mother to my grandmother to the life I believed I was leaving behind. We stopped for a bite to eat somewhere in North Texas, and after I got Dustin and Amber back in the car with full stomachs, they fell asleep, giving me that selfish time alone I had been wanting. I loved my children with every bit of energy, but looking back at the kid I was, I can see that I didn't have much energy to give. We crossed into New Mexico and my first reaction was *Shit! I'm lost. I'm not supposed to be in fucking New Mexico.* I glanced at the atlas and saw that I was on the right track. Tired is the only explanation I had as to why my mind wasn't working correctly.

I was thirteen hours into my trip, only halfway, when the sun started to peek in my rearview mirror and cast a yellow glow across the sky, bouncing back into my eyes from the mountains ahead. Turning the dial, I found the only clear radio station, blaring classic country through the speakers with the occasional interruption from the DJ talking about the weather. "Who gives a shit! You just told us five minutes ago that it might rain!" I yelled at the dash. Clearly, I was hangry. I pulled into a small roadside café and woke up the kids.

I'm sure the coffee was generic, and the food was a day old or two, but that was the best breakfast I had had in a long time. Dustin and I joked about the different colors of the semi-trucks in the parking lot and blew into our chocolate milk through straws, creating bubbles that spilled out onto the table. I got the energy I needed, along with forgiveness from my children for being a bitch the day before we jetted off to California.

After driving all night through in uncharted areas, and now finally in the last eight hours of the trip, you'd think I would be ok. I didn't realize turning north onto a two-lane highway that the gas station we passed would be my last chance for fuel for miles and miles. But I managed to blow by the last station and of course, I didn't realize it until the light for low fuel came on. The kids were awake, and I didn't want to alarm them, but the greatest fear swept over my body. I had made it too far to run out of gas in the middle of nowhere. I had no cell phone, and thoughts of all the horror movies I had seen about young women running out of gas in the middle of Bum Fuck Egypt flooded my head. I tried babying the car on hills in hopes to save fuel, and I started crying for the fear of being stranded.

Rounding a corner, actually the last corner I thought I was going to make, a bright orange Phillips 66 sign greeted me. It was an old station with only one pump, but as long as they had gas I didn't care. An old man walked out of the white screen door from the station, wiping the sweat from his forehead with a blue bandana. "Fill'er up?" he asked with a good ole thick Southern accent.

"Yes, sir," I said through my tears.

He chuckled, "No need to cry, sweetie. You made it." He said it as if it were a reoccurring theme for that part of the country.

A full tank of gas and only forty dollars left, we finally pulled into Sacramento and an extreme feeling of relief swept over my body. I rolled down my windows allowing the kids and myself to breath in the fresh air of Northern California. Traffic was more than I had expected, but I didn't care.

Thoughts drifted through my head about my grandmother and the stress I must have put her through leaving in such a rush. But turning down the street that Angel and Robby lived on erased any worries and gave me a sense of accomplishment that I had just journeyed across our country with only my two kids.

Angel opened the door to their four-bedroom house to a very tired small family excited to start their lives over in California. We unloaded the car and quietly walked in, trying our best not to wake Angel's infant. They had recently welcomed a newborn and Angel graciously offered to keep my kids while I searched for work.

During the long drive out, and having time to calm down, I knew I owed Rob a call and excused myself to their kitchen, where I dialed my grandmother's number from their phone. I knew with Rob being a felon he would want nothing to do with the law, and he knew that I would call the police in a heartbeat if he pushed me. To my surprise, we had a civil call. I told him that I didn't want my life to continue down the path with him and he seemed to be content with my decision. We agreed that in a couple of months he'd come to visit, but we would move on and start our separate lives.

Angel and I became close and, on many occasions, we would take the kids to a nearby park and watch them play while gabbing like sisters. Exploring Sacramento and living with people in a non-turbulent relationship had quickly sunk into my lifestyle and every day that passed made California seem a better choice.

There were many job opportunities, but with a lack of a high school diploma and under the age of 21, I came up short. I rolled up my sleeves and walked into the industry that I was becoming familiar with, exotic dancing. Once I found a club, Angel helped by watching the kids at night, and I raked in the money, putting back everything I could to move out and get a place of our own.

Chapter 12

Rob had called a couple of times to check on the kids and of course check up on me, and after a few times of him asking for them, I started mulling it over. *How in the hell could I live without my kids? How could a mother just pass off her kids?* My mother had done this several times, leaving a toxic taste in my mouth about me doing the same.

"Let me come get the kids and give you time to get settled," he said.

"And how long is that going to be?" I answered.

I heard him laugh on the other end of the phone. "It's you we're talking about; you'll probably have their college paid for in three months."

A smirk crossed my face. I could make a shitload of money without them to worry about. And if we set a time frame . . . "Three months from the time you pick them up, then I come to Arkansas and get them," I ordered.

"Three months, and if it makes you feel better, I will move in with your grandmother. I don't have anywhere else to go."

"Deal." I took it like we were negotiating a used car deal.

I remember the day Rob came to Sacramento to pick up the kids, it was like one of those fucking feel-good movies that has a bunch of sad shit in it. I kissed the kids and helped get them in their seats. I leaned up and squared up to Rob. "Please take care of them. If anything happens or if this isn't working out, I will come to Arkansas and get them."

He placed his hand on my shoulder, the touch making me cringe inside. "I got this."

They drove out of the driveway waving and didn't stop all the way down the street. My gut began turning over and my heart started racing. A lump formed in my throat and I could feel everything coming up. *Holy shit, what have I done?*

I cried as if I had lost everyone in my life, and in a sense, I had, but that evening, something changed: my mind, my emotions, and my sense of responsibility. I had practically been homeless from eleven to sixteen, fighting for my life, pregnant at sixteen, married at seventeen—I had never had time to myself. The phrase "sowing your wild oats" had come to mind a few times, and that is exactly what I did.

The following night, I was dancing at the club and hustling a couple of guys who were loose with their money. I stepped off the stage and stopped at the bar for a glass of water. "Damn, girl, you are working it tonight," the DJ replied, also getting water for himself.

"What do you mean?"

"You're doing great," he replied and turned to customer.

Toward the end of the night, the DJ handed me a bottle of water. "I'm Lonnie." He stuck out his hand. I sized him up, trying to figure if this was a pickup. "It's just water." He smiled, giving me some relief.

That one conversation started a great friendship for my time in California and gave me someone other than Angel whom I could trust. For the next couple of months, we spent time like we were an old married couple, and many people who saw us out believed we were in fact married. But we were just friends, and Lonnie was just a good guy.

The summer nights were warm, and with San Francisco only thirty minutes away, Lonnie and I made several trips. We partied at night and went to tourist sites during the day. I was able to tell Lonnie everything about myself and my life back in Arkansas. He just listened. One night I stopped myself in mid-sentence while walking in a mall. "Why are you being so friendly me?"

He laughed. "Can't a guy and a girl just be friends?"

No! This was something foreign to me, a guy who didn't want anything, a guy who wasn't going to take advantage of me. *Men can be nice?*

We went to baseball games, movies, and bars, living a crazy life, but as time grew so did my motherly instinct; I missed my children. I had made it two months, two weeks and three days without my kids when I called Rob back in Arkansas. We agreed for me to come back and get the kids.

The plans were for me to dance two more nights and put back another thousand dollars to rent an apartment and gather some furniture. Sharing the plan with Lonnie, I was surprised by his answer. "I'll go with you. Drop me off in Oklahoma City so I can see my parents, then pick me up on the way back through. I would hate for you to make the trip by yourself."

The next day Lonnie and I climbed in the car and headed east.

Chapter 13

With the hits of 1998 blaring in the speakers and the windows down allowing Cali air to push through the car, Lonnie and I jetted across the mountains on a two-lane highway. The landscape was dry and bare with tumbleweeds racing each other to the next barbed-wire fence, but I never noticed—instead, my mind was on the two little kids I was racing to pick up. We skirted past Las Vegas and the thought crossed my mind about dancing in a casino. But with super strict laws and extremely competitive girls, I was happy at the two-stage club in Sacramento.

The plan was to stop somewhere between Albuquerque and Amarillo, but the high of seeing my kids after two-and-a-half months of "living it up" pushed our car onward to Oklahoma City. "You sure you don't want to stay and get some rest?" Lonnie asked in his parent's driveway.

"I'm good," I assured him while backing the car out. It was only a four-and-a-half-hour drive, and after eighteen hours on the road, that was just a hop, skip, and a jump. I wheeled into my grandmother's street in North Little Rock and the memories flooded my mind like a soldier returning home from active duty. Good memories were trumped by the bad, and the decision to move my kids out west was solidified.

The car never made it into park before Dustin dove off the front porch, yelling "Mommy's home!" Is it wrong that I wanted to correct him that this wasn't home? Nevertheless, hearing his voice and seeing his precious face was the perfect end to a very long trip. A long trip that I would retake the following day.

In the short time I was there, it was great seeing my grandmother and my uncle, but the memory of the chaos and the abuse from that home made me cringe at the thoughts of the past. Rob was kosher, but I stayed my distance – I wanted to grab the kids and head back west. The following day, I couldn't get out of that house and North Little Rock quick enough, even though I only got three hours of sleep.

In Oklahoma, the kids met Lonnie for the first time. I was grateful that he offered to drive, and you bet your ass I let him. Dustin woke me up close to dark. I felt like I had been asleep for days. Four hungry bodies raced into a Cracker Barrel. It was more than we wanted to spend, but with a toy section in the store, it was a great babysitting venue. "Are we in a hurry to get back?" Lonnie asked.

"Not really."

"Let's get a room and stay the night. It would be stupid for us to drive all night."

I agreed. We got a room with double beds and Lonnie slept in one and the kids and I slept in the other. Not the greatest idea, since Dustin loves to kick in his sleep. I think I got another three hours.

After a quick breakfast the following morning, we were back on the road. The drive was long, and we stopped for a late lunch or an early supper, depending on your take of a 5 p.m. meal. I hadn't eaten since breakfast, and I scarfed down a large meal before offering to drive.

We were close to Modesto, only 130 miles from our destination when a sleeping sensation swept over my body. A heavy meal and no sleep aren't a good combination. Lonnie was asleep in the passenger side, Amber, who was 2, asleep in her car seat, and Dustin, who was 4, lying across Lonnie and me in the front seat. Me? Asleep behind the wheel!

People say that before you die, your life flashes before your eyes. That's bullshit. I felt a floating sensation and opened my eyes to a swirling vision. A swirling vision because I had managed to drive off an embankment of an overpass, and our car was flipping end over end.

Witnesses claimed that I was swerving across the lanes just before driving off the side of the highway. My car landed on its hood after tumbling seven or eight times. I couldn't move, I didn't know where I was—I was completely disoriented until Amber cried out from the back seat. Tangled in my seatbelt in the front, I was just barely able to look back and see her hanging from her car seat, screaming my name. Confused and dazed, I reached back and unsnapped her seatbelt causing her to fall out and break her collarbone. Then panic hit.

"Dustin!" I screamed while pulling Amber from the twisted backseat and shattered glass. I scanned the front and backseat the best I could, but through her crying from the pain in her shoulder and someone pulling me from behind, I didn't see him. A stranger pulled me to my feet, and another helped get Amber out of the car. "Dustin!" I continued to scream.

"Is there someone else in the car?" I heard the stranger ask me, then ask the other person.

"I don't see anyone." the other person replied.

Frantically I continued to scream Dustin's name, scanning the area. "I think you're in shock. There isn't anyone else here," the man told me, trying to calm me down.

Like a scene plays out in a movie, everything was in slow motion, and as the dust settled, things became clear. I looked beyond the crumpled car and saw a small sneaker resting above the grass. I pulled away from the stranger and circled around the car to bring a sight into view that no mother should have to see—my four-year-old son lying face down in a grassy ditch. I sprinted to his side and slid up to him on my knees. "GOD NO! GOD NO! PLEASE, PLEASE DON'T TAKE HIM FROM ME!" God wasn't going to take my son. I couldn't allow it.

Dustin moved his arms and began crying as he came to. I rolled him over with the help of the strangers and collapsed beside him holding Amber. I don't have medical training, but with Dustin screaming and holding his leg, there was no doubt it was broken. I sat on the grass holding my children, refusing to let anyone else hold them, and then a state trooper appeared in my face. "Were you three the only ones in the car?"

I'm sure I looked as confused as I was. "Yes." Then it hit me. I looked at him. "Lonnie."

He jumped to a stand and gazed out across the area, then I saw him point at a body more than thirty feet from the car. Lonnie's body.

There lay a man who just wanted to help keep me company on a long drive, who gave me the first glimpse of what a safe man looked like, joked with my kids like a sweet uncle, and was my first male best friend.

I knew by the reaction of everyone that I had killed him.

Paramedics made it onto the scene, tending to my children and me, and with everything happening so fast I wasn't able to see what they were doing with Lonnie. I did see them load him into the helicopter, his head swollen twice its normal size and his eye with no signs of life. *Why would they fly someone who's dead?*

"How is Lonnie?" I asked a female paramedic.

She looked at me and through a half-smile replied, "Let's get you and your kids in the ambulance and to the hospital."

Chapter 14

"**M**ommy, are we going to jail?" Dustin asked me with the siren from the ambulance howling through the city streets. It was a strange feeling that my son related flashing red lights and sirens to being in trouble, but with the last three years and how many times the police had come to our place, I could understand.

"No sweetie, we are going to the hospital."

"Ok." Dustin leaned back in the stretcher, then looked back at me. "He said I would be ok."

"Who did?" I asked.

"The man that wrapped me up while I was flying." Chills ran up my spine. Part of me wanted to ask who, but only an angel could have saved my boy.

I patted him on the arm. "And you are ok." I smiled, trying to comfort his pain. I couldn't shake the vision of

Lonnie as they had loaded him in the helicopter, head swollen and blood running down his arm. I paused for a moment. *God, take care of Lonnie.*

They wheeled the three of us on stretchers into the Emergency Room. It was obvious that word of the wreck had reached them. Nurses, doctors, and aides scurried to our sides trying their best to help comfort my children who were crying with a panic tone.

A state trooper followed me into the small room. "I didn't mean to fall asleep," I confessed with guilt. "I ate a large meal and we've been on the road for days," I continued to plead my case.

He raised his hand. "No one is to blame here; I just have a couple of questions."

After a few simple and generic questions, he wished us luck and started out. He stopped himself by placing a hand on the door frame and turned to face me. "I've seen a lot of wrecks in my time and this one should have taken each one of your lives. You guys are a lucky bunch."

"Thank you," I softly answered.

He smiled at Dustin and then at me. "If it wasn't for your male friend wrapping up your son as they were ejected from the car, I truly believe your son wouldn't have made it."

I stared at him like a ghost had walked in. "Lonnie?" I asked.

"Yes, ma'am. In our investigation, we figured that while the car was rolling, Lonnie grabbed your boy. Seatbelts save lives, but in this instant, an Earthly angel named Lonnie saved his." He pointed at Dustin. I should have been arrested for not having my child buckled in a car seat. What was I thinking of letting him out? Parents please keep your children in their seats at all times.

The man whom I felt the safest around was my son's Earthly guardian angel. It was the voice of my friend that my son had heard while flying in the air, it was his reassuring words that had given Dustin comfort. I had never been around a hero or even known what a real hero looked like, but I give thanks to Lonnie almost every day I see Dustin's face. To this day, the wreck haunts me more than all the other bullshit that has plagued my life.

We didn't see Lonnie come through the ER. I asked a nurse about him and learned that he had gone straight to surgery with severe head trauma. After X-rays on Amber's shoulder, we were told that it would heal on its own, but for my little boy's leg, surgery would be needed in the next day or two. *Shit! What else could go wrong?* I shouldn't have asked, because Angel walked in holding her cell phone with Rob on the other end.

I was, however, surprised at his calmness and quick action. "I'm on my way," he told me over the phone. I had a plan. I was going to raise my kids in California, we were going to live in an apartment, and we were going to be happy. But I lost all my common sense and needed someone to lean on, and that person happened to be Rob.

We stayed with Angel and Robby while Dustin went through surgery. I was a mess and needed help. I didn't mean to lead Rob into believing that we were going to make up; it was the last thing I wanted, but for those few days, I couldn't think straight.

Lonnie went through multiple surgeries in a short time period but thankfully he pulled through. The first time I saw Lonnie I broke into tears; he was cover in stitches that closed the wounds from the wreck. "Don't cry Jeanette, it's not your fault. Plus, these scars will add character," he replied.

Rob and I picked him up from the hospital and took him to his house, where a couple of his friends had planned to stay with him and help him recover. In my numbness and still partially confused, I said goodbye to him and climbed in the car with Rob to head back to Arkansas.

It was just for a short time and we'd be back in California . . . Lonnie and I would be able to spend more time together . . . we'd be able to continue this great friendship that we'd started . . . but my life isn't that simple. In fact, I never returned to California. I can explain that in a little while, but first I have something to say to my son's Earthly angel.

Lonnie, I am truly sorry that I never returned. I am sorry that I didn't keep in touch over the years. There isn't a day that goes by that I don't think about our friendship. Dustin is now getting married and starting a family of his own. There are times I see a reflection of you in his eyes, a reflection of someone who is honest, true, and genuine.

I miss you. Thank you for being that angel. Thank you for saving my son.

Chapter 15

By nature, I am a planning person—my schedule, my future, my finances, and other important things. We weren't over the state line of California and I was planning my next trip back. I wasn't going to stay in Arkansas, there was no way in hell. I had an unfurnished apartment in Sacramento and had already scouted the schools for Dustin and Amber. But Rob was now talking about us moving back with him. I had a taste of living away from family and the slums of North Little Rock, and I had zero intentions of moving back, especially with him. I kept my mouth shut.

The kids sat in the back of the Ford Ranger with seats that faced each other, sleeping as much as they could. Dustin's leg was propped up on a stack of bags and Amber was strapped in her car seat. We all had on our seat belts.

We were on Interstate 40, also known as the Purple Heart trail, in the middle of nowhere, when Rob pulled over. "You need to drive."

Drive? I just almost killed everyone a week ago and now I'm expected to drive? "Rob, I don't want to drive. I don't think I'm ready."

"I don't see any hotels here, and unless you want to sleep on the side of the road, you will drive," he demanded.

"Rob," I started to plead with him.

He put his hand in my face. "Get your fucking ass behind this wheel and drive!"

There he was! That was the Rob I was used too. I wasn't going to press the issue, so with my stomach in knots I climbed over and slid behind the wheel. I looked in my rearview mirror before pulling out.

"There isn't anyone around for miles, go!" he yelled, then scrunched down in the seat, pulling his trucker hat over his eyes.

Just drive and get through this, I told myself over and over. I would get back to Arkansas and get Dustin well with the help from my grandmother, then head back. I steered the Ford Ranger down the desolate interstate with the background of dried vegetation and bare mountain tops. I glanced out the window, thinking that I had allowed my life to look much like my surroundings, but I was totally convinced that I was a fighter and the only thing that would beat me was death itself. Funny I would think that as Rob made his next statement.

"I'm thankful you're coming home to me," he replied under his truck hat.

"I'm only coming home to my grandmother, and once Dustin is healed, I'm bringing them back to California." *Why in the fuck did I just say that?*

He lifted his hat with the forefinger of his right hand. "What?"

Well, I'm in it this far—I might as well tell him. Right?
"Rob, I don't love you. We aren't getting back together." *Jeanette! Shut your damn mouth*, I thought to myself.

Rob violently reached for the wheel and yanked it downward, causing us to fishtail at seventy-five miles per hour. I slammed on the brake causing everything in the truck to shift to the front. We came to a stop in the middle of the Purple Heart Trail.

Now, I have gone through a lot of physical pain in my life—sport injuries, fights, the wreck a week before—but what I felt next hurt unlike anything I have ever felt. Rob's right fist crashing into my jaw jarring my sight and dazing me long enough for him to get four more blows into my face and rib cage. I opened the driver door, unbuckled my seat belt, and fell to the asphalt.

Surely someone is pulling up to stop this. Surely I am not the only one on this highway. Surely God isn't this fucking cruel! And maybe it was God's punishment for thinking that. Rob made it around the truck, and with my two babies watching from the back seat, he continued to beat the living shit out of me. "You're coming home to me no matter what!" he screamed, inches from my face.

I felt what little I had in my stomach trying to come up, but the punches he had landed and the kicks from his boots in my gut wouldn't allow it. I spit on the road, bright red puddles of blood. I ran my tongue over my teeth, checking to see if they were all there. Thank God I had all of my teeth.

"Now get in the truck and shut them damn kids up!" He pushed me back to the driver's seat. I looked back at Dustin, and through a spiraling vision, I asked them to please be quiet, told them that Mommy was going to be ok.

I looked forward and couldn't see straight, and with fear in my voice, said, "I can't see."

"Well shit! Get over here and I'll drive." He stepped out of the passenger side and I quickly jumped over so I wouldn't be hit again.

I would not have changed seats with him if it weren't for my two kids in the back seat. During that moment, I wouldn't have had any trouble driving us up to a hundred miles per hour and crashing us into a giant rock or something.

Shit! Who am I kidding? There is no way in hell that I would have let that son-of-a-bitch win over me. I was born a fighter, have been fighting ever since—this day and shit like this made me who I am.

We got back to North Little Rock and lived with my grandmother while Dustin's leg healed. With the help from my grandmother watching the kids at night, I danced at the club, and I mean danced my ass off. I put away money that Rob had no clue about. In the exotic dancing world, there are a few elite clubs where dancers make up to $125,000 a year and one of those clubs happen to be two hours east of Little Rock, in Memphis, Tennessee.

On a fall night, while Rob was driving a truck somewhere in south Arkansas, I packed up what little belongings I had and stepped out onto the front porch of my grandmother's house. The kids and I kissed her goodbye, the relief in her eyes was as clear as the sky that night. We drove east on a two-lane country highway, the opposite direction of California, with the stars above guiding our way. I spent most of the time peering out of the windshield at the light above, and with a calm and peaceful sensation, I knew we were going to be ok.

Chapter 16

Everything seemed to happen in a flash—arriving in Memphis, signing the contract to our new apartment, the delivery of furniture, and other things that come with moving to a new place. We hadn't been in Tennessee for forty-eight hours and already I was so disconnected from home it seemed like years since I had spoken to anyone. Looking back, I really believe that I had gone through so much shit that I had developed the ability to block out the past. That sometimes worked to my advantage but would later come back to bite me on the ass. But for now, life was good.

We had rented an apartment in the southern part of town, what I still believe is a great place to live. I had owned my own house, which I lost during the shit with Rob, and lived the American dream. Living in the apartment complex gave us amenities that I hadn't had before, a gym to work out, a pool, and two playgrounds.

Our apartment, number 216, was extremely new. I'm not sure anyone had lived in it before us. I can remember, upon walking in, the smell of new carpet, new paint, and new cabinets. Could it be a prophetic sign of a new life? I mean, we had an upstairs, and only rich people had two floors. And the staircase was covered in new carpet, something that became an entertainment area for my little family.

"Mommy? Is that our bedroom?" Dustin yelled from the top of the stairs.

"Yes baby, it is." *And how in the hell did you get up there so fast?* Dustin was still in a full leg cast from the car wreck, something that continued to haunt my dreams at night. I was the reason that he was on crutches, the reason for his full-length cast, the reason he struggled to bathe at night so he wouldn't get his leg wet. It's hard to let go of things when they involve your kids.

I was unpacking what little things I had in the kitchen when I heard the scream just seconds after Dustin asked about his room at the top of the stairs. I pulled myself around the corner of the hall from the doorframe in pure panic that he had fallen down the stairs. And sure enough, there was Dustin at the foot of the stairs. Not crying but laughing. I stood confused long enough for him to pick up on my flight into the hall.

"Mommy, you gotta see this." He turned and hopped on one leg back to the top of the stairs. Amber jumped in my lap with a fully entertained expression. I was still dumbfounded about their excitement until I watched Dustin slide down the carpeted stairs on his makeshift sled: his cast.

Amber screamed with laughter, and to this day I can remember the joy that was painted all over my kids' faces. I couldn't do anything but roll over in laughter with my children, and Dustin did it over and over, causing us to laugh harder and harder. You don't know how good it felt to just laugh. It had been years, too damn long. For the first time in a very long time, my children and I were just laughing and over the funniest sight I had ever seen.

We had stepped up into the upper class: new apartment, new town, new life, and within the next couple of days a new place to work. We spent our time touring the town and the parks that were scattered through the city limits. One park, in particular, our favorite, was Shelby Farms. We could spend the whole day there and never get bored, and between the playgrounds, the zoo, the waterfronts, and the endless amount of green grass, we were just happy. To this day, it is still one of my favorites, and it is this park that I owe gratitude toward for giving me a complete sense of peace and happiness, something I never had before.

If you know Memphis and you are a foody, then you know of the many places we ate and had some of the best experiences. From throwing toothpicks into ceiling tiles to devouring the best BBQ in the country, I loved the restaurant

scene of Memphis. My kids, they loved good ole McDonald's.
I mean, Dustin's first word was McDonald's. But they
enjoyed other restaurants, we weren't ever hungry, and the
greatest thing was that I could afford it.

I could afford it because I was finally in a high-caliber
club that attracted the top dancers from all over the South,
along with men with deep pockets.

On a normal night, the club hosted 200-300 dancers, and
on special nights with special guests, the count would be
closer to 400 exotic dancers. Each girl would pay fifty dollars
to dance every night, so the club would make around $12,000
to $15,000 dollars just from them on an average night. That's
not including the door or the bar. Yep, this club banked it
every night the doors were open.

Dancing on stage would always land some pretty good
money, but where the dancers made the most were lap dances.
Each girl would charge $40 a lap dance, and I would always
give 25+ lap dances a night. Do the math and you will find
that it adds up to $1,000 per night. Not bad for four hours of
work. Many nights, I walked out with $1,500. 300 girls at
$1,000+ is over $300,000. You can't tell me there isn't some
crazy money in the exotic dancer industry.

But in all cases that I have found in life, money doesn't
make you happy and exploiting yourself naked on stage for
fantasizing eyes to linger on certainly doesn't.

Chapter 17

My life was becoming like the story of the prostitute who was picked up one night in a sports car, hired for a week, given lavish clothing and sparkling jewelry, and ended up marrying her knight on a white horse. Sound familiar? It should. *Pretty Woman* was a box office hit that glorified the lives of prostitutes. It also gave me the presumption that I would be met with lights, alluring music, an attentive audience, and US currency floating through the air, softy landing at my feet. *Pretty Woman* was also criticized for shining a false light on the life that torments women who are slaved into an industry. Exotic dancers aren't that different.

I remember my first night at the club. I parked in the back with all the other dancers and walked to the door where I was instructed to knock, and someone would let me in. I was so nervous that I stopped three or four times thinking this was wrong, but the thought of money forced me to the door. I knocked and the door was opened by one of the bouncers, who smiled and welcomed me like I was a celebrity. Another lie. When he shut the door, déjà vu raced through my mind with the sound I had heard from my first club, the sound of a jail cell slamming shut.

One of the owners, that I had interviewed with, happened to be walking by. "Well hello, Jeanette. We are excited to have you here tonight."

I couldn't believe he remembered my name, but it gave me some sense of peace knowing that they had heavy security and a personal staff. I paid my fifty dollars to a lady and then made my way to the dressing room. I had been around long enough to know that if I walked in timid, the other girls would pick up on it, chew me up, and spit me out. So, I entered the dressing room with an attitude and a demeanor like a pro. They didn't mess with me.

Working was hard! My first night I felt like a truck had run over me and backed up to finish me off. I hadn't ever given that many lap dances in one night and the muscles in my legs let me know. I also felt like eyes were watching me from the management, so I wanted to be as seductive on my last dance as I was on my first. But at the end of the night, walking out with $1,200 in my pocket helped with the soreness.

There is a romantic allure from the secular side of this world that exotic dancers are displaying their beauty created by God. The curves of hips and legs, the shape of the breast, the tightness of an ass, all something to celebrate like a nude painting from Botticelli. Bullshit! Nudity is nudity, and displaying it is driven by the selfish desires of selfish people.

Don't agree and want to argue? Try me!

I spent years enslaved to nudity, not because I wanted to be a piece of art, but because people paid me. Dancing and displaying yourself for tantalizing thoughts were nothing but a big gamble of self-worth. Any dancer would agree with me, or they are still hypnotized by the lie we were all fed.

Dancing was a drug. I loved it at the moment and desired more of it, but at the end of the night, I would leave through the back door and walk the walk of shame to my car. I had to learn to endure the ignominy that followed me for days after I would dance. It was like a hangover. The fix? Do it all over again and let the money and acceptance from men drive the lie I was living.

On nights that I didn't make my goal, I would leave with the struggle of low self-esteem, feeling that I wasn't pretty enough or sexy enough to attract those standing in the crowd. But it was nights like those that drove me to work harder, dance harder and go beyond the boundaries of our lap dances.

Then there were nights I would show up for fifteen minutes and anxiety would set in and mentally drive me away. I questioned myself every day, but I couldn't stop.

Honestly? I never thought I would be writing my story with my seventeen-year-old daughter downstairs watching TV. I never thought that my life would have an impact on my kids. I'm not sure if we are taught by society or if it is a learned behavior that we never think about the consequences. I fought for survival growing up and was forced to make decisions based on necessities. Looking back, I might have taken a different path. But that is hindsight, and my life has defined the person I am today.

It was important for me to explain my past to my children, not for their approval to share my story with the world but to share with them that there will always be a better path in one's journey.

Dustin, my oldest, learned of my dancing when he was thirteen years old. I can remember the conversation like it was yesterday. He took it harder than I ever expected, and I never thought he would find himself embarrassed to be around me. Many people in the small town we live in knew of my past, and the others? They know now. Dustin is now in his twenties and starting a family. He sees the need for others to hear my story and gave me his blessing to tell it.

Amber, my middle child, really didn't care at the time. "It doesn't matter, it's your life," was the answer I got from her. Again, not what I was expecting. However, that attitude has changed now that I am writing this book. I've lost some respect from her, but my prayer is that she'll see the lives I am trying to reach.

Ashton? Well, she just found out and is still processing the whole thing. All in all, I would guess she is pretty neutral on the subject. Mostly because she was so young when I quit that it's just a story to her. Amber and Dustin lived through it.

But dancing was part of my life, and I can only hope that my decisions can rescue anyone from that industry or anyone who is thinking about the industry.

My story doesn't end here, though. As a matter of fact, it's only starting.

Chapter 18

It was a Saturday night and unusually slow for the club. I had danced a few times and given maybe a dozen lap dances. Some of the girls had cut out early and had invited me to go eat with them at a trendy place on Beale Street. I kicked around the thought of joining them but figured the fewer the girls at the club the more money for me, so I stayed. It was a restaurant that I wanted to try, but money was more important to me while I was single for the first time in a long time.

The dressing room was quiet and lacking the drama that normally went down, so I took advantage of the somberness and stretched out on one of the couches for a rest. I had just gotten comfortable when one of the dancers busted in the room. "Bunch of money-carrying fraternity fools just walked in."

It was kind of code for "There is money up for grabs," and since I turned down the invite to eat, I climbed to my feet and walked out onto the main floor. A group of young college guys had managed to push two tall tables together and were ordering drinks. A couple of girls made their pass through the tables seeking lap dances, but they were turned down at the guys' table.

"What's the matter, scared your moms will find out you had a lap dance?" I teased them, putting my arm around two of the guys.

"How do you know that my mother doesn't work here?" one of them popped off sarcastically.

"That would make you an elementary or maybe middle schooler? But hey, maybe mentally you are," I popped back.

His frat brothers laughed, one of them giving him a shove on the shoulder, telling him he had better keep his comments to himself, there wasn't any winning against me. One of the guys that was sitting back like he didn't want to be included spoke up and asked what a lap dance cost. I looked at him for a moment, then replied, "Wait, I know you." The table fell out laughing at my comment.

I wasn't trying to be funny or witty—I really recognized him from somewhere, I just couldn't put my finger on it. Then it hit me, I knew him from him dating a girl that I knew. I pulled up a barstool next to him and we talked for the next couple of drinks. I figured he had enough alcohol in him. "Do you want a lap dance?"

"Sure," he casually answered.

"How about one in the VIP lounge?" I upped the stakes. The VIP lounge was a minimum of $250, but it didn't seem to faze him. He dropped over $300 cash on the table. I grabbed his shirt and told the table that we'd be back later in the night. Guiding him to the lounge, I turned to him and formally introduced myself. "My name is Jeanette, and you are?" *Holy shit! Did I just give this guy my real name?* It was something I never did. Dancers use a stage name to help hide their identity, and it was considered a cardinal sin to give your real one. I had just committed that sin.

"Jeff," he answered.

We spent the rest of the night in the VIP lounge with a dance here and there but mainly sat and talked about life. There was something about him—he was easy to talk with and presented charm and chivalry, something that I wasn't used too.

Toward the end of the night, I did something else that was totally against my rules and the rules of the club—I gave Jeff my number. He left with the other guys and I was certain that he would call, but after a week I chalked it up to being completely stupid. Then, on the eighth day, my phone rang, and it was him.

He explained that his friends were coming back to the club and he'd like to see me again. Not what I had in mind when I had given him my number. I was thinking of maybe, "Hey, you want to go eat?" or, "How about a date?" not, "You want to strip for me again?" But I figured I had learned a lesson on why I shouldn't give my number out. Time to hustle now!

"If my friends go to the club would you be interested in grabbing a drink or maybe supper instead?" Ok, I ate my words.

"Sure, I guess we can."

I knew how to play the game. While his friends gave all their parents' hard-earned money to a group of exotic dancers, I went out with Jeff. And that is where our relationship started. Over the next few months, he would come to Memphis and we'd hang out, go to the parks or the movies, listen to bands on Beale Street, and watch football on TV, a sport that I'd learn to hate.

It was during a Sunday game at my apartment that he dropped a bit of big news on me—it turned out he was going to be a father any day. He explained that it had happened during a one-night fling, which I found out later that wasn't entirely true. Then he asked me to meet his parents, who lived in Chicago.

They were visiting him in Russellville, Arkansas, the town where he went to college. The following day I dropped the kids off with Rob, not daring to tell him that I was going to meet my new friend's parents, and Jeff and I made our way two hours west.

It was awkward meeting them at his place, but it was even more awkward when his mother asked how we met. At this point in my life, I was making a shit ton of money, fully independent, and didn't give a shit about anything. I thought he was going to pass out when I answered, "We met at a dance club in Memphis."

"Like a strip club?" his mother asked, with her eyes wide open.

"Yep."

"What were you doing at a strip club?" his father asked.

I could see the warning in Jeff's eye's but again, I didn't really give a shit. "I was dancing," I said proudly.

"Is there good money in that?" his father asked, surprising me.

"I make six figures a year and work three nights a week."

He smiled at his wife. "We need to get these two married and that boy off my wallet."

Everyone laughed and the conversation went from awkward to sweet and uplifting. I thought he was just joking about getting Jeff off his wallet, but I later learned there was a lot of truth in that statement. Jeff's parents were from a high-society life in upper Chicago and carried a flare of wealth but never looked down on me. Over time they learned of my past and the hell I'd been through and believe it or not they gained a level of respect for me. Something that nobody had had for me. Not many people had treated me in that manner, and it felt good.

Looking back, I can see that they pushed our relationship thinking that I was best for Jeff and that I was someone who could take care of him.

During our time dating, I traveled to Russellville two or three times a week, dropping my kids off between Rob and my grandmother, whom they dearly loved. Jeff's daughter, Kelsea, was born during this time, and it took a while for her mother to accept me, but when she did, we actually became good friends.

And Kelsey's feelings toward me? This is what she wrote just the other day for my forty-first birthday.

HAPPY HAPPY BIRTHDAY TO THE BEST STEPMOM I'VE EVER HAD!!!

I'm sorry my text is late, I got caught up in all kinds of schoolwork today. I hope it's been an absolutely wonderful day for a woman that's more than deserving of it.

There is more, but that's just between us. Suffice to say, after eight months of dating, I married Jeff and moved to Russellville.

Going too fast? Hang on!

Chapter 19

Weddings are meant to be a sparkling day with the air filled with floral aromas, jitters, unruly nerves from the mother of the bride, and hungover groomsmen from the night before. Well, the groomsmen were definitely hungover but the rest . . . well, let's just say my wedding day was a tad different. But let's back up.

Jeff was still in school at Arkansas Tech, where he was a grad assistant for the football team, meaning he was an assistant coach's assistant. He had played for Tech his freshman and sophomore year, ending his football career with a severe back injury he'd earned in practice. With the sport still flowing through his veins and the passion to remain involved, he turned to the next best thing to playing; coaching.

I, on the other hand, had no idea what coaching entailed and certainly didn't know what being a coach's wife meant.

There were long evenings of sitting in the bleachers, whether at home or away, and trying to keep two little kids at the age of 5 and 3 entertained for three hours was a whole different story. The coach's wives all sat together and for all I know traded cooking recipes and homemaker tips. Or they could have been selling fucking drugs or pimping out—I know that they weren't interested in including a GA's soon-to-be wife. I sound upset about it, but trust me, I wasn't. I was lonely going to all the games.

No matter if they won or lost, Jeff was always pissed off after the game. "They played like shit! If I was out there, we'd never have done (this or that)," he would bitch. I never knew what he was saying and never learned the lingo of the sport—I didn't really give a shit. And trust me, after sitting through a full season of hot-ass fucking weather to colder-than-a-witch's-tit weather, I learned to hate the sport.

Jeff's parents weren't really too interested in football either, and the few times we spent with them before we married, the subject hardly came up. I can say the one thing I did enjoy was every Saturday before the game when we would go eat at the same country buffet restaurant, and every time I would order grilled pork chops and Jeff would eat grilled fish. I do miss that.

After the season, they ended up winning their conference, which was a great resume builder for Jeff and one of the reasons he landed his first job coaching in Searcy, Arkansas, thirty minutes closer to Memphis.

But before we moved, we got hitched!

I had spent the entire football season reading bridal magazines in the stands and watching my kids. I knew what flowers I wanted, the cake design, the type of paper for the wedding invitations (which was handmade seed paper derived from cottonseed found in the Southern states and super eco-friendly). I had planned every minute of our day and every little detail that any bride would die for. I had planned the original good-old Southern traditional wedding with God, government, and all to witness. What I got was extremely different.

Jeff's parents helped with the wedding, and with their deep pockets, we booked the Searcy Country Club, a place like I had dreamed about as a little girl. I think all little girls dream and practice their wedding day—I mean, it's the day we all get to marry our Prince Charming. And to quote *Pretty Woman,* "I get to be Cinde-fucking-rella."

We picked our groomsmen and bridesmaids mostly from his friend list and thought we put together a group of fun people. The night before the wedding, some things went on between the wedding party that I shouldn't mention. I shouldn't . . . but I'm going to! Jeff and I excused ourselves early from the party to go get some rest, something that I was desperately needing. And let's just say hooking up was what happened. I wasn't there, so I don't know the details. I can say that during the ceremony, both sides kept their heads down and never made eye contact. That is, the ones that showed up for the wedding.

The day started out warm for a December Saturday, and thunderstorms were in the forecast. I was standing in the doorway looking out into the parking lot, waiting for my grandparents to drive up. My mother would have been there with the exception that she was on house arrest for writing hot checks and drug charges. My grandparents showed up late because they were involved in a hit and run, totaling their vehicle and leaving them stranded and sore from the crash.

Pacing the bride's room, I could feel everything falling apart and my dream day coming to a crashing end. Then, to make things worse, one of the bridesmaids' mothers came in to wish me luck. I didn't need luck, I just wanted to have a nice wedding. She leaned over to kiss me and somehow got red lipstick on my white dress. Holy shit did Bridezilla show up in true fashion!

First, I'm sorry to the bridesmaid's mother. Damn good thing I wasn't into Voodoo, because they'd have all been up the creek without a paddle. Second, I was having the ultimate meltdown until my hero of the day walked in. My stepfather.

This is the kind of man my stepfather was—he didn't attend the reception because they were serving alcohol, and he had made a promise to his church not to attend functions with alcohol. I respect the hell out of that.

After the photographer miraculously got out the red lipstick, she lined my stepfather and myself up in the door to walk down the aisle. That's when I noticed I was short two bridesmaids. Then Dustin and Amber, my two precious children that could never do anything wrong, broke out into a fight halfway down the aisle because Amber wouldn't throw any rose peddles. The wind picked up outside, the skies darkened, the wedding march began to play, and the tornado sirens went off throughout the city.

"Stay in your fucking seats! I'm getting married," I wanted to scream to the crowd, but the smile from the pastor standing by Jeff told me to keep my mouth shut. Jeff's side of the room was full, with a couple hundred people showing up to support him. My side? Mostly empty. And actually, some of Jeff's friends and family members were embarrassed for me, so they switched sides to try and even out the room.

Through all of this cluster, I felt my stepfather's arm tighten, and glancing over into his eyes, I saw him smile, giving me the sense of peace I desperately needed.

Then it hit me! I'm getting married. This is my day. I'm in a beautiful dress. There are flowers lining the aisle, the cake was perfectly designed, and each person here had received a handmade invitation. All the hell I'd been through, all the negative comments said about me, the uninvited hands when I was a child, the lies I had believed, and the support I never received—it all disappeared for this day. I was beautiful, and I felt it. I was the queen I had dreamed of being.

Chapter 20

We married so close to Christmas that we didn't take a honeymoon. Instead, we drove nine hours north to the windy city, Chicago. I had seen snow before, but I was taken aback the farther north we drove and the deeper the snow collected along the interstate. I had been in traffic before too, but how in the hell do people in Chicago do it with bumper-to-bumper traffic for miles? Our nine-hour drive turned into eleven because we didn't plan our trip wisely and drove into the city limits at 5 p.m.

Thank God I packed snacks for the kids because there was no pulling over for food, and with our windows fogging with the brutal temperatures outside, we finally managed to pull into Jeff's parents' neighborhood. Craftsman-style houses lined the street, with each one casting a flare of difference from the next. Parking in the driveway, I would have kissed the concrete, but it was too cold.

Jeff's mother opened the door and greeted us, "Come in, come in before you freeze."

The kids and I walked in their home to a fire in the fireplace, soft music playing in the background, and the aroma of food drifting through the downstairs.

"Hope you guys are hungry. Just grilled some pork chops," his father announced from the kitchen. I grinned at Jeff, who just rolled his eyes, knowing that grilled pork chops were my favorite. You would have thought we hadn't eaten in a week because our butts barely hit the chairs before everything was scarfed down.

Our time with his parents was fun and a needed break from the rat race in Arkansas with my family and my commute to and from work. I believe it was the model of his parents that helped us into a routine life, something that lasted maybe three years.

On the third evening we were there, I turned down a trip to the mall with Jeff and his parents and stayed behind with my kids to have some alone time. Dustin was being a little more rambunctious than normal, so I thought it would be a good idea to go outside and have a snowball fight. This lasted maybe five minutes, and with frozen hands and faces, we raced back to the front door to get by the fire. Only thing is, I didn't know the door locked when we went out. I could barely see my cell phone on the coffee table, all nice and warm. *Why didn't I bring it out here?*

"Mommy, I'm ready to go in," Amber said in a sweet and soft voice.

"I am too, honey. Let me figure this out." I smiled at her. Being a Southerner, we didn't own cold-weather clothes, and my kids had no clue what thermals were.

"What do you mean figure it out? Are we locked out?" Dustin's voice grew louder. "We're going to die out here!" He fell back into the snow, being dramatic.

A pair of headlights crossed the front of the house and I turned to see Jeff and his parents coming back early. "Don't say anything," I instructed them.

"It's mighty cold to be outside." Jeff's mother said, walking back up to the house.

"We were just about to go back in," I assured her.

Jeff's father opened the door and let everyone in, and as I passed through the doorway, he made the comment that it was good their trip was cut short. I replied with the statement, "I don't know why, I had it under control."

He laughed.

Back in Russellville, Arkansas, life was normal for us as a young family. The kids went to school, we worked, we lived in a small house, and we had two cars. The American dream, right? Well, with the exception that I was an exotic dancer who drove four hours to and from work three times a week. I would wake up and get my children off to school, get Jeff off to his school and GA job, and leave our house at noon, then drive to Memphis and drive back and get in bed at 3 a.m. I was like a machine—it didn't faze me; I was too hung up on the amount of money I was making. I just didn't realize we were spending so much at home.

I never looked at the commute as a negative thing, and over the first few years, I befriended another dancer who let me stay at her apartment to help cut down on the driving. I was kind of like an invisible roommate; she put herself through school and became a nurse working during the day, and I worked at night. We were never at the apartment at the same time.

I worked my ass off and supported our family as Jeff continued his education toward his undergrad while coaching as a GA. We got his daughter, Kelsea, every other weekend, and I did my best to make sure I didn't work on those weekends, giving us time together. And Kelsea's mother? The one-night fling? She'd actually been Jeff's fiancée. I learned that after we got married. And actually, we became good friends over time. This was something that always made Jeff nervous.

And wouldn't you know it, during our busy and crazy schedule, I managed to get pregnant with my third child, Ashton. As a dancer, you only get paid when you work—no dancing, no pay. And I figured I would only have five months to dance before I started to show. That's five months of working twice as much to put back enough money to get us through childbirth and pay the bills.

Time flew, and within five months I was working the floor at the club when one of my regulars stopped me and made the comment that I was glowing. He was glad to see that I was happy. "I am happy, but I'm not glowing because of that. I'm five months pregnant," I told him. You would have thought I ran over his favorite cat because he just stared at me.

"Girl, you need to go home and have that baby. You don't need to be in a club pregnant," he lectured me.

"Yea, you're probably right," I answered him, and I drove home that night, not to return to the club for four months and two weeks, and dead-ass broke.

Chapter 21

Like I said previously, in my line of profession, if you don't work you don't get paid, and going four or five months on the money you have saved isn't easy. In fact, it wasn't possible for me, the only provider in the family.

Exotic dancers who perform at a high, professional level don't just jump up on stage and shed their clothes. Skin care, dieting, body toning, and cardio exercise are all musts. That means expensive skincare products, eating clean and healthy, gym memberships, personal training, and in many cases plastic surgery. Implants are not cheap, and when I had that procedure, I didn't have thoughts about pain or side effects, my main thought was, *Why I didn't go to med school? Oh yeah, no structure or education. I just wish I had a normal job that I could be proud of.* When you're making $1,000+ a night, most of these things are affordable. Not so much while pregnant.

Jeff and I didn't fight over many things, but one reoccurring fight was money. I was a saver and he was a spender. And I kept a budget. It wasn't something that somebody taught me or sat down and showed me, it was something that I did to keep up with our spending. It caused fights, depression, and questioning of career, but it saved us in the long run.

It was a Sunday and close to noon—I knew that because some of our neighbors were pulling up in their driveways and climbing out of their recently washed cars wearing their Sunday best when my phone rang. Looking at the screen, I saw it was Jeff's grandmother, Jo. I had met Jo at the wedding and in Chicago, and with her carefree and happy attitude, I fell in love with her.

"Hey, Jo. How's life in Chicago?" I asked.

"It was good until today," she replied. Then she continued with a story of how Jeff's parents were asking her to move out of their house and find her own place. In a nice way—at least I hope it was.

"Where are you going?" I questioned.

"I don't know," she said with a tone between sadness and defeat.

"I know! You're moving in with us! And please say yes, I need you." I didn't mean to sound so needy. What am I saying? Of course, I did.

"Do you need to talk with Jeff?"

"Don't worry about Jeff," I said. "I am sure he won't mind."

I stood in front of the washing machine, running over in my mind how I was going to break the news to him when he walked in. Everything I had practiced in sixty seconds went out the window. "Your grandmother is driving down here today and moving in with us." I didn't give him an ultimatum.

"What are you talking about? Are you serious?" he asked like a weight had been lifted off his shoulders.

"Yep, and we both know we could use the help around here," I said, with Jeff fully agreeing with me. Not too surprising.

The following day, Jeff's grandmother, Jo, moved in with us, and I can assure you he was extremely happy. I like to think that it was because he loved his grandmother so much, but part of me knew it was because he would have less work to do around the house. And yes, she helped with the kids, my crazy pregnant moods, cleaning the house, and staying on Jeff's ass about spending so much money.

Our house backed up to the playground of the school Dustin attended, and I can't explain how easy it was to get him ready for school and watch him walk through the back yard and past the jungle gym, disappearing into the school doors every morning. It is a beautiful sight that has been embedded in my mind and something I won't let go of, even though he's in his twenties now.

Jo was in her mid-seventies when she moved in with us and had been retired for several years. Jeff and I fought less with Jo living with us. She loved to help and took a lot of stress off me.

The third pregnancy is supposed to be easier, right? Nope, just as hard as the first two and sleep was something that was a struggle. I slept late and Jo was more than willing to help get Dustin off to school and take care of Amber until I got up. Jo was a busybody; she even organized my dancing clothes out of boredom. What grandmother do you know would organize an exotic dancer's clothes?

Chapter 22

It had been a month since Jo moved in, and I can't emphasize enough how much of an earthly angel she was helping with everything. I'd have to say Jo didn't put up with a bunch of shit from her grandson, she made him work. Our house had to have been the cleanest one on the street, both inside and out.

One morning, I woke up earlier than normal and went for a short walk to catch some fresh air and got back around 9 a.m. I know this because I heard the second bell ringing from the school. I don't remember where Jo had gone, maybe to the grocery store or the dollar store, but I remember she had already left. I heard the back door close, but it didn't slam, like everyone in the family would let it.

I snuck around the corner and examined the room and the back door, which wasn't completely closed. "Hello?" I called out, almost in a whisper. Not sure if it was the hormones from pregnancy or the horror show I had watched the night before, but I got a funny feeling in my gut. "Jo?" I prayed she would answer.

Nothing.

The house was dead quiet. Too quiet. I tiptoed down the hall and pulled open Amber's door to check on her. She was four years old and beginning school the following year and very easy to raise, but one thing was wrong—she wasn't in her room. *Maybe Jo took her with her.* The thought dashed through my head. *That's stupid, Jo would have told me.* I walked back into the living room and paused. Still, no Amber.

Then the fear of the horror movie started becoming reality. Someone had entered my house and taken my daughter. *That's stupid too. I am going crazy, she's around here.* I walked throughout the house, checking every room and stopped periodically to listen for the sweet voice that she used when she talked to herself or her imaginary friend. I stopped to regather my thoughts, and that's when panic set in. I dialed Jo's number but didn't get an answer. I dialed Jeff's number, but it went straight to voicemail.

I walked out to the front yard, somewhere Amber never played, and glanced down the street to my left. Nothing. I glanced to the right and caught the glimpse of a white minivan turning the corner. Why is it that kidnappings always include a white van? Or maybe that's my imagination, too. I freaked and ran down the street, screaming Amber's name and chasing the van that was now well out of sight. I sprinted back to our carport to get my car when I noticed something missing in the garage—not our car, but Amber's tricycle was gone.

Ok, stopping freaking out! I coached myself and struggled to put two and two together. In the past few weeks, I had let Amber follow me on her tricycle to the school to get Dustin, and now it was starting to make some sense to me. I jogged out of the house and through the playground, heading to the front of the school and the place I always picked up Dustin. Lo and behold, there was Amber's tricycle on its side near the front door. I raced inside to the office holding my belly, where I was met with a room full of smiling faces. "I believe little Miss Amber came to check on her brother in class. I was just looking up your number to call you," the secretary welcomed me.

Before I was able to catch my breath, I saw the principal walking with Amber down the hallway and toward the office. "Hi, Mommy," she said, walking in. "Bubba is ok." It was a name she called her brother.

"Hello, Jeanette. Someone is overanxious about starting school." The principal handed off my daughter.

"Holy cow," I finally spoke, a little surprised I didn't have more colorful words to say. "Thank you, this won't happen again."

"It's ok, I'm glad she didn't get far," he replied.

We walked back to the house, slowly allowing Amber to ride her tricycle and stop and pick every little flower along the crumpled sidewalk. I couldn't believe that I was a mother who'd lost her child and let her imagination take over—I struggled for years hoping that if a real situation came, I wouldn't freak out. But, watching her pick white and yellow flowers and handing them to me for safekeeping put me at ease for her safety and wellbeing. At least until she became an adult, but real mothers never stop loving no matter what, and putting husbands (real husbands) and children first in our lives is what we are programmed for. Something my own mother never understood.

Amber and I reached the house in time to see Jo pull up in the drive and climb out of her car with a paper bag from the store. "Where have you two been?" She smiled.

"Just walking the sidewalks," I answered, playing off the incident. Amber snatched a few of the flowers from my hand and ran to present them to mama Jo. She explained how she had gone to the school to check on Dustin and how she managed to pull every flower between here and the school.

Jo smiled at me with a strong, telepathic "been-there-done-that" thought that only mothers can understand. They disappeared inside while I remained in the backyard, looking at the school building that protected my son. A playful kick came from my belly I said in a soft voice, "I will always be here for you, no matter what." The kicks slowly settled and I am sure she fully understood that I would always be there for her.

Chapter 23

It had been four months, three weeks, and two days since I walked out of the club in Memphis, I struggled with the money we had left. Jeff was finishing his under-grad and with neither one of us working we were running out of money and getting behind on bills.

It was a Saturday morning and I was sitting at the table, internally bawling over the stack of bills that was steadily growing. "You going to pay those?" Jeff walked in, not even looking in my direction.

I pealed the top layer off the stack and started rummaging through them when I came across our gym membership. "This can go," I said aloud, and looking back I wish I would have said anything else.

"I don't think so." Jeff snatched the $50 bill out of my hand.

"You don't go."

"I think I'll start back."

"Don't you have the gym at the school to work out in if you wanted to?"

"Doesn't matter. I say what stays and what can go," he started but was abruptly stopped by me.

Now to get something out in the open. I am controlling. I don't deny it—in fact, I vocally own it. I had also made $125,000 a year working three days a week. Jeff wasn't working. And please understand, we were broke and I was extremely stressed out.

"Who the fuck do you think you are talking?" I cut my eyes at him, and for the first time since he had walked into the kitchen, we made eye contact. Jo? She left.

"Excuse me? I'm the man of this house," he snapped back.

I took a deep breath and decided this was going to be a civil argument. I gripped the table to prevent myself from throwing something at him. "I have given you every opportunity to be the man of this house, but you have a spending problem. We are out of money. We can't afford the wants. Gym, cable, phones, and other things are just going to have to wait until I build up our account."

"Yea, right." He walked out.

Well, fuck being civil! The shit hit the fan. It started in the kitchen, made it to the bedroom, into the living room, and out into the front yard. We've had some good fights, but this was the big one. I wanted so badly to leave, to climb in the car and drive far away. California, Memphis, North Little Rock— anywhere but here.

I stood barefoot, shaking in anger and tired of screaming. The thought of running flooded my head, like a little devil on my shoulder coaching me to the car. Is this what my mother had faced her whole life? Was this the same devil that caused her to run, to turn to drugs, to sleep with strangers, to abandon her daughter? God, it would be so easy. But I'm not my mother, and if she taught me anything in life, it was to not follow in her footsteps.

Jeff climbed into the car and peeled out, leaving me standing in the driveway with a half-dozen neighbors watching the scene unfold. I wiped the tears from my face and returned to the house to hear Amber crying in her room.

Dustin met me in the hall. "Mommy, you ok?" He could see the tears that hadn't fallen from my bloodshot eyes.

I smiled. "I am." I patted him on the head and pulled Amber up into my arms, then took them to the living room to watch Saturday-morning cartoons.

I was so mad that at the time, I didn't care if Jeff came back or not. One thing was clear to me: I wasn't going anywhere. I wish I could say that things got better, but in fact, things got worse, much worse. We did run out of money before I could make enough at the club. Jeff's parents loaned us money, so we were able to buy groceries and diapers but not enough to pay for our house.

During the following days, we stressed, argued, and cried about meeting the end to our money. Jeff had graduated college and had placed many resumes in the state but hadn't heard anything back. One afternoon we were sitting on the couch when he opened a congratulations card from his parents, a check for $1,500 fell out. A big sigh of relief rushed through my head, knowing that we could eat for the next couple of months, pay a two-months-past-due electric bill, and receive some much needed peace.

However, for a celebration, Jeff and a couple of his buddies left the following day with the $1,500 burning a hole in his pocket, and they disappeared to a small casino town in Mississippi. Easy come and easy go, right? Jeff gambled all $1,500 away with drinks in one hand and who knows what in the other. I sat at home, unaware of his celebration, with two children eating mac and cheese and watching whatever station we could get on the makeshift antenna I had made days earlier.

It was just after 2 a.m. when I received a call from Jeff, explaining he had totaled his vehicle on the way back from the small casino town.

"You were where?" I asked, confused.

"I've been celebrating my graduation with my friends in Mississippi."

"How did you pay for this trip?" I asked.

"With my money my parents gave me."

"How much do you have left?"

"Lost it all on one hell of a night," he announced, proud.

I hung up.

Chapter 24

The following week, I didn't speak to Jeff, and for the most part, I didn't acknowledge his existence. Jo understood and completely agreed with me, but continued to help with his clothes, cooking, and other household chores I wouldn't do for him. We managed to coast through the month on what little we had from the money we borrowed from his parents. Jo helped a little, but living on a fixed income, she didn't have much to offer.

With Jeff's resume he was hired in Searcy, Arkansas as the middle school PE teacher and soccer coach. We left our college town where I didn't have to hide my profession, to a town where I did. Here I felt like I had to hide my profession and act like the other young housewives. It was harder than I thought.

Searcy was new to me, it was hard to meet people, plus I had just had my third child and was busy with her and the other two. But I had been there long enough to learn that Searcy was a bible-beating Southern town with the church ruling over the government, educational system, and social life of 90 percent of the population. Something very new to both of us.

It was August when Jeff received news about his job and even though I was still pissed about him blowing the money for graduation, I was happy for him. We celebrated his new job and the move with burgers on the grill and cold beer and mentally took a deep breath of fresh air.

Two weeks after having Ashton I picked up jogging to help get my dancers body back. Jeff's job was a relief for our financial situation but we both knew that in order for us to get ahead I needed to return to the stage.

I had never graduated from high school, and with Jeff holding his bachelor's degree, it made me want to achieve something, too. I enrolled in an online course and started studying to get my GED. I didn't need it . . . or rather, I thought I didn't need it, but it felt good.

"Hey, babe!" Jeff busted in the front door one afternoon after practice.

"In here," I answered, feeding Ashton in the kitchen.

"We've been invited to a BBQ with the other coaches and wives," he smiled.

I blew the hair out of my eyes. "When?"

"Tonight," he answered with a bigger smile, then left the room.

I looked at Ashton, then at Dustin, who was busy coloring in a book, and then at my old t-shirt and sweats. "I can't go tonight; I don't have anything to wear. . . My hair hasn't been cut in months and . . ."

He cut me off. "Just put on something and we probably should take something."

My left eyebrow raised with the thought of his audacity to just assume I could throw something on and whip up something with a twitch of my nose. (Bewitched Pun – for you post-1970s people). But I had to take into consideration that I was married to a simple-minded, barbaric caveman.

Two hours later, and with much help from Jo feeding the older kids, I walked out of the bedroom wearing jeans and a long-sleeve t-shirt. I glanced in the mirror that hung in our living room. *Why is it so hard to get my dancer's body back*, I thought.

"Damn babe, you look great," Jeff said, surprised.

I really want to be mad at Jeff, but he continued to bail himself out, and one way to make me happy is to tell me I look pretty, even though we both knew different.

We drove through the small historical part of downtown Searcy and out by the park on the way to the head coach's house. I gazed out at the families in the park playing with their children and felt guilty that we weren't one of them. Turning down the street, I could see three cars parked in front of a nice house, and three other coaches and their wives walking with sides dishes and desserts, dressed to the hilt.

Now, I was really feeling self-conscious about my appearance. I was normally in tip-top shape with a body built like a brick shit house. I mean, it was my profession to look the best, and when you dance on stage three nights a week, six times a night, and give forty-plus lap dances, your abs become like ribs of steel.

I'm not trying to give anyone ideas of becoming an exotic dancer to better their body. There were also perverted men who would grab my breasts, my ass, and on occasion my crotch. And of course, they were gently tossed out of the club by a six-foot-eight male bouncer any time I lifted a finger, no questions asked.

But I was going to make the best of this for Jeff, so I put on my smile and followed him and the other three couples. Now, I don't know if those girls felt like I did or were just scared, but they didn't say anything and kept their heads down, walking behind their husbands. Not me—I reached for Jeff's hand and walked into the backyard.

This was an annual party where all the coaches, both high school and junior high, came together with their wives. I wasn't sure who was who and just stood back and listened to everyone talk like they had known each other for years.

"You must be Jeanette?" A lady maybe in her forties approached me.

"I am," I answered, confused, not realizing that Jeff had talked about me with the other coaches. It turned out she was the head coach's wife and the host of the party. She was sweet but busy talking with other wives and explaining where to set each side and dessert everyone had brought. I latched on to her conversations and learned quickly that I wasn't the only new wife amongst the group. Turned out that most of the wives didn't know each other, they were just really good bullshitters.

I soon found myself in a small group of girls talking about kids, being a coach's wife, and what they did in their spare time. "Jeanette?" One of them pulled my attention back to the conversation from the chocolate pie that was sitting five feet away.

"Yes?" I smiled.

"Do you work?"

"I do," I answered before I had time to think about the question.

She followed up with a question I wasn't prepared for. "What do you do?"

It was probably just me, but it felt like I stood there for hours with a blank stare, not knowing how I should answer. Kind of like the Hitchcock movie scene where the person stands still and the surroundings fade back. Time seemed to crawl while six coaches' wives stared me down waiting, patiently for my answer. "I flip houses for a living," I said, taking a sip of my drink. Their mouths fell open with impressed expressions. *What the fuck! Where in the hell did that come from? Flip houses? Why in the hell did I just say that?*

"That's really cool. Do you have your own crew?" she followed up.

What the fuck is a crew? "I sure do." *Holy shit, I am getting deep into something I am not used to.* But what could I have said? "I am an exotic dancer in Memphis who entertains single and married men three to four nights a week." I don't think so, not in this bible-beating church-ruled town. Plus, Jeff would have been looking for a job before sunrise. I created a lie that I had to live with for nearly three years before . . . well, we'll get to that.

Chapter 25

Three months clicked by and I found myself in October in a town that didn't believe in Halloween, just Fall festivals. It was also mid-way through the football season. Outside of my lie of flipping houses and my disappearances three to four times a week to Memphis, I started feeling kind of normal, like I was becoming a real person. I was a mother and a football coach's wife—I was just missing something, something to feel complete.

By now, Jeff was doing great at his coaching job and proudly hung his college diploma on the wall. Me? Two-and-a-half years of high school—I had missed my opportunity at any type of education.

My life was all a disguise. I dressed modestly, I hung around educated people (during football season), and I even had a faux job of flipping houses. All in all, anyone who knew me during this time of my life and lived in Searcy would have known me as a normal wife. What they didn't see was the blinding lights on stage, the revealing dresses that left little to the imagination, the seductive lap dances, and the six figures that bought our home. Still, I wasn't happy, I didn't feel complete.

The girl whom I had been staying with from time to time in Memphis had battled her way through her GED and nursing school, all while sharing the same stage with me at nights. I didn't need my GED to push into the faces of others or to put a patch on my jacket. It was something I needed personally, private, something just for me.

I was spending mornings getting the kids off to school and then, with a table still filled with half-opened cereal boxes and spilled milk, I concentrated on schoolwork. Work that I had missed as a pregnant sixteen-year-old.

Days rolled into weeks, and with determination, perseverance, and a shit-ton of broken pencils, I managed to complete my GED. A weight lifted off my shoulders, and with a victory dance in the kitchen and a dramatic jump, spin and twirl, I tabbed the enter key to my laptop and sent the final part of my schoolwork. No one was home, no high fives at the finish line, no fireworks and confetti, no popped corks of champagne, and no roaring of an overexcited crowd, just me and the most accomplished feeling I had ever experienced.

Like in that movie, *The Christmas Story,* I waited impatiently by the mailbox for my version of the Little

Orphan Annie Decoder Ring, AKA my diploma. I had been to the store and bought three different picture frames to make sure I had the right one when it came. And on one cold afternoon, I spotted the mailman stop at our mailbox and fold a large envelope to make it fit in the mailbox. I knew it was my diploma; I walked quickly to the mailbox, trying not to look suspicious to the neighbors or anyone else, and pulled out the folded envelope.

I wasn't upset with the mailman for folding it. I was too excited to receive my accomplishment. I went inside and pulled out the letter along with a golden-laced certificate. Tears formed in my eyes, and for a short moment I thought, *this is stupid, why am I getting emotional over a GED?* But those thoughts were extinguished as I picked out the right frame and proudly propped it on the table for everyone in the family to see.

Jo was the first, and like all amazing grandmothers, she shared my excitement with hugs and kisses. The kids were kids and didn't have a clue what a GED was. Then Jeff came home.

"See anything new?" I made a gameshow wave toward the table.

"Oh yeah, good job." He walked past me and into the kitchen. I don't know what I was expecting, but still, I picked up the frame and started to place it on its designated spot on the wall. "Are you hanging it up?"

"I am," I smiled.

"It's just a GED. Anyone can get one." At first, I ignored the comment and proceeded with the hanging. He continued, "Babe, don't hang that up. It's embarrassing."

I'd been kicked, punched, and even cut with a glass bottle, but I had never felt the sharpness of a stainless-steel blade before. The coldness of the metal, the sharpness of the pain as it passes through each layer of muscle, and the agony as it passes through the heart. No, I wasn't stabbed, but it felt like it. My diploma found its home in the bottom drawer of the kitchen.

I had come to learn how to forget the digs, insults, and painful remarks of the person I shared a bed with, but this one never left my thoughts.

With my GED tucked away for no one to see, I started searching the local wanted ads in the paper and the internet for anything in small-town Arkansas. One afternoon, I found an ad in the paper that a local bank was hiring. I caught Jeff as he walked through the house. "Do you think I should apply for this banking job?"

"I don't know. Does it pay as much as the club?" He left the room before I could answer with a no.

Though his question made my skin crawl with anger, I couldn't help but think he was right—there was no way in hell I could top my club money. I mean, the president of the branch I was applying for made less than I did.

I built a resume from a template that I found online and dressed in the most casual business attire I could put together and drove to the bank. There was a place online to submit resumes, but I was determined to hand mine in personally. I worked a "personal" job at the club and doubted there was any other greater relational position than what I had do in the past.

As I marched into the bank, a lady in a black dress and wearing high heels met me at the door. "Welcome, can I help you?" she asked.

"I'm here to turn in my resume for the position."

Her expression turned cold as she eyed me up and down. "Oh! You'll have to apply for that online. Sorry." She turned.

I noticed a sharply dressed man exit one of the offices in a fast-paced walk. I knew how to read people, and I knew "who was who" by the way they walked. This was the boss. I slid past the rude lady and approached the man. "I know this might be unconventional and I should do this online, but I am more relational than that and wanted to hand this in in person."

"I tried to explain that to her," the lady started to defend herself, but the man stuck up his hand, cutting her off and reading over my resume.

"I like that, boldness and going out of your way. Personal is what we are looking for here." He glanced over my shoulder at the lady. "Give her an application."

"Yes, sir."

He looked back at me. "When can you start?"

Chapter 26

Jeff and I repeatedly had problems, and there were occasions where I had left him for short periods of time. Unfortunately, our arguments and separations bled into the lives of others, and soon we become "that couple" among the football wives.

I'm not sure if it was really that bad or if it just gave the other wives time away from their problems. Nevertheless, I was the talk when they would congregate. I was still trying to live this normal housewife with a banking job life by day and being an exotic dancer at night. I was hoodwinked into thinking that I could keep up the charade of living a double life but looking back I now realize that people were figuring out my true identity.

I believe it all came out when Jeff said he was going out with his buddies one night. I had put the kids to bed and climbed in bed wearing sweats and a large, long-sleeve t-shirt.

I had to dress seductively for my job; I sure the hell wasn't going to dress that way at home. I stayed up reading a book about running and when I glanced at the digital clock on my nightstand, it was 2 a.m.

Where is he? I picked up the phone and called Jeff but didn't get an answer. I turned out the lights and tried to go to sleep, but horrifying visions flooded my head. Not that something had happened to him—the thoughts were of him with another woman. We hadn't been the model married couple and had had our fights, but the thought of him with another woman turned my stomach.

Yes, I was a stripper at night, gave many lap dances, and let men drift off into their fantasies, but I took my marriage serious. At least as much as I could when seduction was my job. A few of the nights out of football season I worked, Jeff would come with me and sit in a corner, watching sports on his phone. It was just work and something we had agreed wouldn't come between us. Let's face it, he enjoyed the money.

Him with another woman? Different story. I was more exhausted than I realized, and before long the morning sun broke light through the mini-blinds and onto my closed eyes. I rolled over and saw that it was 8:23 a.m. I tried calling Jeff, no answer.

A hole had grown in the middle of my stomach, and my hands shook as if I was getting over a bad hangover. Then a

roar from oversized tires on a truck turned down our street—I
knew the sounds of his truck better than he did. I flung back
the covers on the bed and stormed to the front door. He
staggered out of his truck, still drunk from his night out, and
walked into the house. "Jeanette, I don't need to hear it from
you right now!"

Excuse the fuck out of me? You bet your ass he heard it
from me! Just thinking back to that morning has my heart rate
up and my blood boiling.

I was under the impression the partying and frat days
were over. He had a family at home and a great career and
was becoming a popular coach in the small town we lived in. I
was so ready to tear his ass up like a parent would a rebellious
child, but this was husband and wife. I really don't know what
frustrated me more, the worrying or the inconsistent
relationship. I know I screamed at him long enough for several
of the neighbors to walk out to check out the commotion. And
long enough to tire myself out—all I wanted to do was go
back to bed. But my mind wouldn't let me; my mind was
planning out the future without Jeff.

I packed up my belongings once again, along with my
kids, and with tears shared with Jo, I left Searcy and made my
way back to the town where I knew I could make it, Memphis.

At first, it felt great to be back, but reality set in, and with
three kids and a nightshift job, things turned tough. I was
paying someone a hundred dollars a night to sit with my kids,

and when I would come home, I was so beat that I just wanted to sleep. Weeks turned into months, and my robotic physical state of sleepless nights started to change me. For the first time in my life, I felt like I was breaking down.

Food didn't taste like anything, my kids were tugging on my last nerve, and I couldn't make enough money to make me happy. I hadn't ever experienced a panic attack. I've lost my shit a few times but never had stress lead to anxiety problems. It seemed like it was just around the corner.

But on an April night, months after I had left Arkansas, Jeff walked back into the club. He sat in the booth where he had waited for me night after night while I worked. One of the other dancers walked past me. "You have a visitor," she said, pointing to the booth. I nodded that I had seen him and continued to entertain one of my regulars.

Glancing over my client's shoulder at Jeff sitting in the booth drinking a beer burned me, not because of the past but because I had trouble resisting him. He had been texting me for the last week, and it was easy to ignore him if I didn't have to see him, but now he was in sight. I wrapped up my lap dance and walked over to him. "Why did you come here?" I asked.

"Please come home," he said, with a hint of remorse in his tone.

Shit! What is it with this guy? Why am I under his spell? I slid into the booth and listened to his sob story of how bad he had it. His story was bullshit and I could see through it like it was a plate of glass, but I still loved him. At least, I thought I did.

Chapter 27

Jeff had pleaded with me, and to be honest, I let him crawl a little before I admitted that I would come home. You could see the relief come over his face, and during that time I thought it was because he needed me, not my money, just me. We went to my apartment and climbed in bed to catch some sleep before we started packing my things.

The kids were surprised to see Jeff walk into the kitchen the following day and seemed happy that we were heading back to Searcy. We hadn't collected much furniture or belongings since all I had been doing was dancing, sleeping, taking care of my children, and then repeat.

Jeff and I picked up right where we left off, arguing about money. I hadn't been home a couple of days and he was wanting to go out with his friends. I hadn't mentioned to him or anyone else that I had to have a small surgery, and in the heat of our argument I belted out, "You want to go out and get drunk with your friends while I sit at home worrying about a surgery I have to have in two days!"

He stopped and looked at me with a blank expression. "What are you talking about?"

"I have to have a small procedure in a couple of days, and I'm nervous."

His voice changed. "Why didn't you tell me?"

"I don't know, I was going to ask Jo to take me to the hospital." During the three months of me living in Memphis, Jo had moved to Benton to be closer to her son, but she was happy that I'd come home.

"I will take you." He pulled out his phone and texted his buddies that he couldn't make it out.

Wait? Who is this guy? Jeff threw me for a loop with his quick mood change. He threw his arms around my head and drew me in to his chest. I was perplexed and speechless with this onset of compassion that I had never seen before. The rough-and-tough Jeanette left, in spirit, and this brittle and emotional person took over my body. I cried.

The next day was different. I can't put my finger on it, but Jeff was definitely acting differently with me. And it went on all day and into the night. I was nervous about my procedure but felt the stress leave knowing Jeff would be there.

The morning of my surgery, Jeff walked into the kitchen wearing his golf attire. "What are you doing?" I asked.

"I have a tournament day with the other coaches." He fixed himself a glass of milk.

Did he forget? He must have. "I have my procedure this morning," I softly reminded him.

He looked at me over the glass he was chugging. "I know."

"You know? Aren't you going with me?"

"You said yourself it was small. You don't need me there worrying you."

"Uh, hello. Yes, I do."

"Sorry, babe. Can't let the other coaches down. Let me know how it goes." He jetted out the door before I could gain my wits.

Holy shit! I just moved back home to this fucking egotistical son-of-a-bitch? I was stunned and paralyzed with the audacity of what I had just witnessed. I lost my mind and in three seconds had already totally convinced myself to cancel the appointment and move back to Memphis when Jo walked in.

"Just breathe," she said, seeing the steam pouring out of my head.

"I can't believe this," I managed to say. She wrapped me up in a big hug, half welcome hug and half consoling hug. Even though she was well aware of Jeff's selfishness, she never said anything negative about him. There was an occasional joke about him not cutting the yard or cleaning the kitchen, but she wasn't one to talk about others in an unsympathetic way.

Jo was the closest person I ever had to a mother. My grandmother was great but had way too many people around who drained her mentally and psychically. Jo was also a strong church-going woman who loved God and loved others. When the doors were open, she was in the pew, and on Wednesday evenings she was serving meals for the weekly potluck dinner.

While living with us, every Sunday morning she would dress in her nicest dress and ask us if we wanted to go. She knew the answer before asking but never missed the opportunity to check. One Sunday morning, she walked into the kitchen and asked. I looked up at Jeff, who just shook his head, and then I spoke up. "I think I will go with you this morning."

Jo wasn't shocked, or if she was, she hid it well. "Come on."

I threw on some jeans with holes in them and a white long-sleeve shirt and followed her out the door. We drove a few minutes across town and parked in front of the Valley Baptist Church where families were unloading, and parents were herding their kids in the doors. As I stepped up onto the sidewalk with Jo, two overdressed ladies popped up in front of us and asked Jo who she was bringing.

"I'm Jeanette. Her daughter-in-law, and I'm also a stripper at a club in Memphis."

You're crazy if you think I said that! Those two old ladies would have stroked out in front of the church, and I don't think God would have let me in. Jo introduced me and we found our seats toward the front.

The singing was . . . well, ok. But the preacher got up and started speaking, and I swear to this day he was speaking to me and only to me. I don't get emotional overhearing people speak but I couldn't stop crying. I know people around me were probably asking themselves what was the matter with her, but I didn't care.

Jo clinched my hand and didn't let go, and that only made me cry more. Then she leaned over and whispered, "God knows your heart, dear." She always made me feel good about myself and filled the hollow part of my heart with her love and motherhood, something I had longed for from my own mother, something I'd never received.

Church was good that day, and it was the start of finding out that something greater lay ahead of me.

That morning, after Jeff left, Jo took me to my procedure, where the doctors ended up determining that I needed a hysterectomy. I wasn't interested in having more children, but at twenty-seven the news hit harder than I had expected. Earlier, I'd felt like my mind was tearing apart; now my body was tearing down, and for the first time in my life I realized that I wouldn't have my dancer's body forever.

Chapter 28

Having spent time in Memphis away from Jeff you can only imagine my bank job didn't last long. At that time of my life, that type of customer service wasn't what I was used to giving—my service was a tad bit different and a little more touchy.

I knew better than to believe Jeff about how things would change; in fact, they went right back to the way everything was before I had left. The only different thing was that Jo wasn't living with us anymore, and I felt like my village had left. I traveled back and forth to Memphis, dancing my ass off and working hard to pay down the enormous debt we had acquired. Long nights and longer drives had begun taking a toll on my body, spirit, and sanity.

Jeff was coaching and teaching PE, bringing home $1,500 a month after his child support. Shit, I often made

$1,500 in one night. As you can imagine, he encouraged me to work harder, saying he'd help with the kids.

"You're a fucking PE coach and you won't teach our kids how to kick a soccer ball," I went off on him one afternoon I was home. He just shrugged my comment off and flopped on the couch, looking for something on TV.

Football season rolled around, and mysteriously I had become one of the veteran coach's wives, even though my marriage was rockier than those of the other wives. I went to the same old preseason BBQ at the head coach's house and met different wives, all with the same deer-in-the-headlights look about their roles.

As the seasons clicked by, I was asked fewer times what I did for a living. I guess since they never saw one of my "flipped houses" on the market, they had figured out that that was a lie. I sure in hell wasn't going to tell them the truth. I just kept quiet around the wives and smiled at their stories about going to the supermarket or bashing their husbands disconnect with their families during football season. Things really didn't change there, either.

But with the help from Jo and the eagerness to make money, I met another man. This man was different—he taught me the value of what to do with all the money I was making. His name is Dave Ramsey, and I went through his class, Financial Peace, at Valley Church.

It was there I learned about putting back cash (into envelopes), having a household budget, paying off debt through a snowball effect, and much more. I had dragged Jeff along, not because I thought he'd have some blinding-light experience about money but hoping that he would finally understand what I was talking about when I would say, "We have to save."

And so, at Valley Baptist Church in Searcy, Arkansas (kind of sounds like a Ray Stevens song, and if you don't know who that is, look him up!) it all clicked with me about the value of saving money. I loved the message Dave shared: that we were not called to be slaves to money but to have complete control over it. And right there, in that small wooden-pew church, I swore to God that it'd be a cold day in hell before I let money control me!

Jeff didn't last long in the class, maybe a few days—he soon came up with an excuse as to why he couldn't be there. But in the long run, he liked me paying bills and putting back for "rainy days." He always said he'd spend it all if he was in charge. I had news for him—he was spending it, even though he wasn't in charge. I had other secrets that I wouldn't tell him, like for instance, in the class, they taught us to put cash in envelopes and spend when needed. When it was all gone, that was it, it was all gone. Well, I had two sets of envelopes for everything we budgeted for, just so I knew for certain we wouldn't run out.

The other secret, I actually started after Ashton was born, was I had a secret bank account that nobody knew about. It allowed me to save money for real emergencies, though thank God we didn't have any big ones. But I had become a guard dog over our finances, and I was pretty damn good at it.

I was a hardcore Dave Ramsey saver, I bought Jeff a Firebird and when he got tired of that, I bought him a Dodge Ram, and when he got tired of that, I bought him another truck. He wasn't complaining. I also danced my ass off with many long nights to buy us a four-bedroom house in a prominent neighborhood.

And with all this free-spending, people in Searcy began talking more. "How can they afford a house bigger than the head coach?" "They must be doing something illegal." Or, my favorite, "She must be prostituting."

Life was getting on track for us and in perfect timing one of my family members called and asked if I knew about one of my cousins attempting to take her life. "What?" I asked over the phone. This young girl was one of my cousins that had lived in the mast population of my grandmother's house during my time there. I drove over to my aunt and uncle's house to find this young ache faced kid in much of the shape I had been in my teenage years.

My heart broke, "Do you care if Rachel stays with us?" I asked my aunt and uncle.

"Nope. If you can help her," they replied.

Rachel reminded me of myself at 15. Jeff agreed to move her in and within a couple of weeks this withdrawn girl blossomed into a beautiful teen full of excitement. My kids fell in love with her and Amber looked up to her like a hero.

With an extra person in the house I was even more thankful for Financial Peace that also helped me with my attitude of people looking in, "I don't give a fuck what they are saying or thinking! I'm debt-free." It felt great, but again I found myself needing something more, something normal, and something I could do to make money when I was too old to dance.

In one of Dave's courses, he talked about how the only investment he never saw declining was real estate. I began looking into things I could do with real estate. Rental houses, buying and selling, or flipping houses (after all, part of this small world thought I was doing that already).

I talked to a close friend of mine who was an agent, and she told me that she loved the customer relationship she had with her clients. That sounded like something I was already damn good at. I signed up to take the real estate exam, and after failing it three times and with a shitload of determination, I passed it and became an agent. Finally, some normality in my life.

Until I found out what people in Searcy knew.

Chapter 29

People didn't learn my true identity overnight—the talk had been going around the town for a couple of years before it really got out. I was dancing at the club four to five nights a week and selling real estate during the day. Along with keeping up with my kids, with the help from Rachel, and somewhere along the way I turned back into my robot self, with little rest, and constantly on the go. Along with all that, as a coach's wife, I was traveling to all the games, appearing at the school functions, and putting up my typical facade.

The lifestyle we were living wasn't making sense to people, and that was the biggest clue that something was going on. I was in real estate and trying to get my start, and Jeff was a football coach—not the typical income to be able to afford new vehicles, a $250,000 house, and nice clothes to keep up with the local lifestyle. As I stated earlier, we were living well ahead of the head coach and his family, something that didn't sit well with the head coach's wife and the others.

I didn't skimp out on my physique either: clean eating, personal fitness coach, and the most skilled hairstylist. In fact, that was where I first heard the rumors.

It was a beautiful, warm Saturday afternoon in the Fall. I was waiting for my hairstylist in the waiting area when two busybodies walked in, talking with each other. "Have you heard?" one lady asked the other.

"Heard what?" the other lady replied.

"One of the school's football wives is a stripper."

"Like on stage, taking her clothes off?"

I almost shit a brick. Have you ever been in a dream when something is about to get you and you can't run or scream? That is what I was experiencing in real life. And as they gossiped back and forth, I wasn't sure if they were directing the conversation at me. They didn't acknowledge my existence or even glance my way, giving me the sense that they were talking about me without addressing me, intentionally.

"My younger sister's daughter, my niece, goes to the school and heard that someone saw her at a club in Memphis. Can you believe the audacity of some people? And living here in our beloved God-fearing town," the lady added.

"Just disgusting! What kind of message is that relaying to our youth?"

"Well, she'll find out what God has in store for her when she's denied the entrance to Heaven and has to spend eternity in hell."

That was it! I was getting the fuck out of that beauty shop, out of that town, and out of the state of Arkansas. That was until my stylist walked in the waiting area and asked for me to come back. And to add to the moment, she turned to me and asked, "How's your husbands coaching job?" To this day, I am not sure why she asked me about my husband, and loud enough for the other ladies to hear. Maybe to shut their gossip down? Maybe to call me out? I doubt that because she wouldn't have cared. Either way, the rest of that visit was awkward with eyes glaring me down the entire time.

I made it home to break the news to Jeff. "You aren't going to believe this," I started before the door could shut. And for the next hour, we deliberated what our story was going to be when the truth came out. Would he lose his job? That was the biggest question, and we finally decided that he would consult the head coach. The devious part of me wanted to be a fly on the wall when the head coach told his wife. But I didn't want Jeff to lose what he had worked so hard for.

I knew how the conversation had gone when I saw his face come back to its normal color. He hung up the phone. "He said I would be fine at my job. He was concerned about you and being shunned in small-town USA."

I was concerned about my real-estate job; I also had worked hard and didn't want to become the leper of the village over my real career. *Maybe this will pass*, I told myself, and went about my day. But that didn't happen.

Apparently, that day, through the big mouth of another busybody, my story got out all over town, and before the start of the following day everyone knew. Shit! They should have just plastered it on the front page of the fucking newspaper.

I went up to the school, not knowing I was the hot topic, to see Jeff and take Rachel a lunch I had made. I walked into a hallway filled with students and teachers. It was during lunch, and I still didn't realize all eyes were glued on me. Not until a cheerleader stopped me, asking, "Are you Coach Jeff's wife?"

"I am." I smiled. She gave me a sinister smile and a nod of approval and pointed to him in the lunchroom. "Thank you," I continued, not sure what to make of her expression.

He met me walking in and quickly walked me back out. "You don't need to be here today."

"Why?"

"They know."

"Who knows?" I asked, knowing the subject matter.

"Everyone." And as soon as he said it, everything in the moment clicked. All eyes, all conversations, all judgement, and all thoughts were directed at me. It was that Alfred Hitchcock moment.

I quickly left and headed to my office with the feeling that the entire town was out to get me. I was that girl! The girl that came to sweet black-and-white Pleasantville USA and brought color. Scenarios played over and over in my mind. *Would I be burned at the stake? Would I be escorted to the city limits and sent on my way? Or would I become the middle school girl with acne and glasses, a loner?*

I had barely gotten behind my desk when a friend of mine walked in and sat down. "Tell me the truth?" she asked.

I might want to add that she was indeed a reporter for the paper. "Yep," I said, trying to act cool.

"What are you thinking? Do you know what the Christian women are going to say about you?"

"I already have heard their snide comments." I stopped and looked at her. "Are you here for a story?" I snapped.

"It would make a good one," she replied with the tone of a vulture circling their prey.

I kicked her out!

Chapter 30

Football season was more entertaining than I had expected now that I was known as the real-estate agent/exotic dancer. The women who didn't know me turned up their noses while their husbands secretively smiled, undressing me in their imaginations. But the women who I did know actually took an interest in my life and let me deeper into their circle. It wasn't what I was expecting from a small town that I thought was run by the Church.

During a Friday home game, I walked in with my kids and Rachel, had several people greet me, and the coaches' wives waved me in for a seat they had saved. My first thought, which was defensive, was what do they want, but that thought disappeared as one of them stood up and gave me a welcome hug. And in front of the entire stands. That was kind of a pivotal moment—the football parents, the fans, the town, everyone accepted me as Jeanette. Well, most people did anyway.

"Jeanette, how's house flipping?" one of the coach's wives asked me with a smile that insinuated I'd had a great front that had fooled them.

"Oh, you know. Busy with contractors," I answered. Then, as if prompted on cue, we all busted out laughing. This was a laugh I needed, and the weight lifted off my shoulders in an exponential way I can't explain.

My cat-and-mouse game was up. I didn't have to lie anymore. But it still wasn't something I publicly talked about. I wanted to shield my kids as much as possible from being labeled. I knew that conversation would come up one day, but until then, I went about life as normally as I could.

My life had become intriguing to the women in Searcy, and any time I was alone with a girlfriend or a woman, the questions came flying. What's it like being on stage in front of a bunch of men? Do you take all your clothes off? What does Jeff think? How's your sex life? Crazy questions. That would almost always be followed up with: Can you give me pointers to entertain my husband? What do you suggest I wear to strip for my man? Do you give dance lessons?

Holy shit, people! I'm not a sex therapist, dance instructor or exotic stylist. And I should say most of these questions came from the housewives, the businesswomen, the churchwomen who initially shunned me when this news broke out.

I understand that women are curious. And looking from the outside, it does have a picturesque and magical flare that could spark a fantasizing imagination. But I was in it for the money. And it takes a very special person to do this night after night and week after week. I'm not painting myself as a super-girl, but it's not all lights and fame.

These women who asked all the questions will never see the hours of traveling back and forth. They won't see the countless men who groped me in areas that only my husband was allowed. They won't see how 99 percent of my customers were really there hoping to get me in the sack that night, to perform for them in their gross fantasies. It was hard work and I was attracted to one thing: money.

Jeff was asked many questions too, some I don't really care to know, but he shared the same belief, that it was only a job. I'm not sure if he didn't gloat a little after the news broke out with the pride that he was married to the stripper. Either way, he was happy about the money. Which is what always led us into our fights.

The dancer part just faded into my name and life, but the fact that my marriage was teetering back and forth was also well-known throughout our small community. Some people wanted to help us and give advice that would save our marriage; others wanted us to just end it because they were getting tired of the off-and-on.

Through the help of Dave Ramsey and the fact that I was OCD about money, I made sure we paid our taxes, used cash for groceries, and lived within our means. This was pretty good with all that we had. I had put a lot down on our house, and we were close to being debt-free, something that was super important to me. That, however, is what led to a horrible fight with Jeff.

Football season had just ended, putting us into the beginning of hunting season, something that most men in the South take seriously. Jeff had a nice ATV that got him around all his hunting leases, but he was hell-bent on buying a new one.

"We don't need another ATV and we are so close to having everything paid for. Can you please wait until next season? We could pay cash for one then," I pleaded.

"I make money too, you know!"

"I know. I am sacrificing many things that I want right now too."

"It's no big deal. I have good credit and can finance it. Maybe $200 a month is all that it'll cost."

"We are almost debt-free. I don't want to finance anything!"

We went to bed that night not talking, barely acknowledging each other. Selfish thoughts poured through my mind about how hard I had worked for our house, the landscaping, a privacy fence, our vehicles, and many other things. I really thought a good night's sleep would fix our argument, but when we woke up the next morning, we just stared at each other.

"Can we put this behind us?" I asked.

"If you're not happy, you can leave," I told him.

It was on our anniversary that this conversation took place, and on December 4, Jeff moved in with Jo, who had moved into a house down the street from us. This only gave more ammo to the gossips of our little Southern town.

Chapter 31

Split up. Again. I spent the day just cleaning and putting things away—it seemed we had let the house get out of hand. The kids and Rachel kept their distance, knowing that the routine of our fights and Jeff leaving the house would put me in a funk. I contemplated throwing Jeff's things out into the street, but I didn't want to alert the neighbors.

Jo called me. "Are you ok?"

"I am, just pissed off. Nothing new I guess."

"You guys need to work things out or just call it quits. You are putting the kids through hell," she preached to me.

"I know." And I did know, I just wished Jeff would see it too. Then maybe we could put this immaturity behind us.

"Let me know if I can do anything for you," Jo replied.

"I will. Thank you and I love you," I said and hung up the phone. Early in our marriage, I would worry to death that Jeff was feeding Jo a bunch of bullshit about me, but as Jo and

I became close, I knew she would let it go in one ear and out the other.

I cleared off the table, knocking a few things to the tile floor. Picking them up, I pulled out a flyer for the real-estate Christmas party. "Well, shit!" I said out loud. *This was going to be fucking embarrassing to go to without Jeff.* Part of myself wished I had waited until after the party to ask him to leave, just so I didn't have to go alone.

Then I remembered I had a dentist appointment. I quickly threw on some clothes and dashed out the door, forgetting my purse. After pulling a U-turn in the middle of the highway and snatching it from the kitchen bar I sped through traffic, trying to make my appointment. I turned in to the parking lot on two wheels and slid to a stop in a vacant spot. I jogged to the door, and upon opening it, all eyes zoned in on me. *What? Did I forget something? Come on folks, the stripper news is old. Haven't you heard? I kicked Jeff out, again.*

"Hi Jeanette," the receptionist behind the desk welcomed me.

It felt good to be noticed. "Sorry I am running late."

"Oh, no worries. Dr. Eichhorn just asked if you were still coming. Have a seat and someone will be right with you."

I turned to take a seat by the TV, wondering why would Dr. Eichhorn care if I was coming. *Is he that anal about people breaking their appointments that he keeps up with everyone?* Something on the TV pulled me out of my thoughts, and just as I was getting into the show, someone called my name out from the door.

Walking through the doors I received a warm welcome from all the girls, even though they knew my occupation. It was a subject that was beginning to dwindle down and be accepted by most of the community. Not all, just most. The hygienists that worked for Scott were never judgmental toward me, something that helped claim my nerves from being in the dentist office.

"Hey Jeanette, how's your day going?" Dr. Eichhorn asked from a small nook at the end of the hallway.

"It could be better." I shook my head. "I'm sorry, it's going ok."

"I'll let my dental hygienist clean your teeth, and then I'll be in to visit with you." He went back to doing whatever it was.

The normal complaint from people visiting their dentist is that everyone wants to talk to you while they have three instruments shoved down your throat. The hygienist that cleaned my teeth was respectful to give me an opportunity to answer questions and me being a talker, I am surprised we ever finished the cleaning.

She finished and made room for Scott . . . I mean, Dr. Eichhorn, to examine my teeth.

"What's up? How could your day be better?" He sat beside me.

"No cavities?" I said as more of a statement than a question.

"Oh, pssh. Your teeth are great as usual. How's Jeff?"

"Jeff and I are separated. He left me." I started confessing like he was my psychiatrist, but Jeff was also a patient of his, and he'd find out sooner or later. I turned to him. "But you know what makes me angrier? I have to go to my real-estate party by myself. Selfish, huh?"

"I feel your pain and what a coincidence. My wife and I split up a few months ago. I guess we have a common issue. Real-estate party? I'll go with you."

I started to unload some other things before it registered with me, did he just invite himself to my party? Did he just ask me out on a date? "I wish I could take you, but that would be too soon for everyone around here if I brought a date."

"I understand." He lowered his head to read my chart.

Holy shit, I can't believe I am going to say this! "But I know another party I could take you to. Want to go to Memphis?"

He smiled. "Yeah, I'd like to go with you."

Now let me say, first of all, he knew I was a dancer. And now all eye's in the office were on him. The mood changed. How could they let their boss, a prominent businessman, and father, go out with a stripper? The beautiful part about this is that his assistances were protective of him, they had witnessed first-hand his separation with his wife. I am sure they had their doubts about him dating a stripper. *And why in the hell was I smiling walking to my vehicle?*

With Rachel watching the kids Scott went with me to Memphis to the club's Christmas party, and I was a little surprised that he fit right in with everyone. I know this wasn't the crowd he was used to spending time with, but everyone fell in love with Scott. We had a great time and a great evening, but the entire time I felt like I was cheating on my husband. And believe me, Scott and I didn't do anything. Not that night.

The following week, Scott and I talked every day on the phone, and as Christmas came and went, New Year's was just around the corner. Scott asked me out to an event in downtown Little Rock, where we had our second date, which went as well as the first.

I was really just having a great time and really wasn't that much into Scott—just for the first time in a long time, I was enjoying someone's company. Someone that I could talk to without arguing or feeling like I was being put down. We kissed at the end of the night and went our separate ways.

The following morning, I received a call from a friend of mine asking if I would come over to her place. I got dressed and sped over, excited to tell her about my date with Scott and ask her what she thought. I parked and walked up to the door, which opened as I reached the front steps. "Hey, Jeanette," my friend greeted me.

I walked in, starting with the news, and then realized that right there, sitting in the room, was Jeff.

Chapter 32

In Jeff's defense, he wasn't aware that our friends had put together this intervention either—I'm really not sure how they lured him to the house. We sat across the room from each other, listening to our friends explain how we had a great marriage and how Jeff was good for my kids and how I was good for his coaching career. I think the only connection Jeff and I made during this awkward time was eye contact and mental telepathy: *Do these people know us at all?*

I sat listening to everyone take turns telling stories about Jeff and myself, and in my guilty conscience, I could only think about how great of a time I had had with Scott. But by the end of the night, they had made a good enough sales pitch to bring us back together for one last try at a marriage that had been doomed from the beginning.

"What do you think, Jeff? Till death do you part?" one of the friends asked. Me? I thought that was the corniest thing I had ever heard, and at that time in my life, death sounded pretty good.

"Yes."

They turned to me only to get a hand in the air. "Don't say it. I'll give it one more try."

In a huge disappointment to everyone, we didn't shed a tear, we didn't kiss, hell we didn't even hug, we just said ok. Stupid Jeanette, stupid Jeanette!

We left that evening, and I followed Jeff to Jo's house to collect his things. I should have taken it as a sign of the future when Jo didn't express any emotions in regard to us getting back together. In fact, I could see the question in her eyes as to why the two of us put each other through so much torture.

He moved back in with the kids and me, trying to make the best of it, and believe it or not we lasted three days.

It was January 5, and we had decided to go to dinner with some friends, a group that had had enough of our offs and ons. We were close to the head coach's house when Jeff proudly announced that he had financed the ATV in our name and that I might see it on my credit report.

No curse words, no violent outburst, not even a raised voice. "I'm not sure how someone can let you finance something in my name without a signature, but I'll fix that. You can pull over and let me out. We are done."

He didn't argue, and since it was a warm night, he pulled over and looked at me. "I'm not going to let you tell me how to run my business," he said.

"And from here on, I won't be there to do that. I expect you to get your stuff out of the house before noon tomorrow," I said in a calm voice.

"I will." And he drove off. I'm not even sure if he went to the party or just to a bar to get drunk.

I had plenty of time walking home to think about everything. I had just told Scott three days ago that I couldn't see him, that I was getting back with my husband. And I had told him face-to-face in his office.

I will confess that part of me thought this would pass. Jeff and I had been in tougher fights than this, and we had made it through much more shit than a stupid ATV. Jeff had had some mysterious spell on me that always lured me back to him, but that night and during that walk, I believe that spell was broken.

Weeks passed by and Jeff and I hadn't spoken a word. Thoughts of Scott began to grow, and guilt also began to fester that I was cheating on my husband with my dentist. After all, my life up to this point would have made a great book, if only it had a great ending. Would that be a life lesson learned through adversity or would that be me riding off in the sunset with Prince Charming? I didn't know at that point in my life.

One afternoon, I drove to North Little Rock to see my grandmother and to seek out any wisdom she had for me. During the years of my fighting with Jeff, working day in and day out and raising my three children, my grandmother had fallen victim of Alzheimer's. The wisdom she once shared with me had dried up between the disease and having shared it with the countless other people and family members she let mooch off her.

She knew who I was but couldn't recall my children or how long I had been gone from her small house. One of the men I remembered well came home while I was visiting, and the thoughts of abuse, neglect, and molestation flooded my thoughts and emotions. "Come talk to me outside." I pulled on my grandmother, but she only looked at me confused. When I told her goodbye, she followed me out crying.

My heart broke watching the lady who'd tried her hardest to raise me cry and wave as I drove off. I felt an enormous amount of guilt knowing that she probably wasn't getting the greatest care, and part of me wanted to turn around and go get her. But if she had been in a strong state of mind, I know she would have said that her home was where she wanted to be.

It was also during this time I realized Jeff and I were truly done. The spell had been broken. I wasn't sure how, but I later found out, and I was released from a doomed marriage years in the making.

I decided to do what I do best. I worked out and developed a kick-ass body, and I danced my ass off making as much money as I could. Why? Because I thought I saw the end of my entertainment days.

Chapter 33

Days turned into weeks and nights turned into days and vice versa, I was selling real estate during the day and dancing at night, working as I had never worked before and absolutely killing it with money. Rachel, who loved the kids, had become their nanny/big sister and helped while I was gone. I was clearing the most money I had ever made, and it only made me work even harder to pay off the vehicles, the house, and a few loans. Not the four-wheeler loan—I'd had my name quickly removed from that.

Jo and I were spending more time together than we had in a long time, and amongst all the motherly love I wondered how my own mother was doing. It had been a long time since we had spoken, and last I knew she was living in a single-wide, rundown trailer somewhere in North Little Rock.

I didn't have time for anyone other than my kids, Jo, and the few clients whose houses I was trying to help sell. Jo had agreed to come over one Sunday afternoon for lunch but called and said she wasn't feeling all that well and asked if she could get a raincheck.

"Of course, I'm sorry you feel bad. Can I bring you over a plate of food or something?" I asked her over the phone.

"No, sweetie, I am going to lie down and rest." She hung up.

Two days went by and I was concerned about Jo, so I called, and Jeff answered coldly. "What do you want?" He must've seen my number on caller ID.

"I'm checking on Jo. I know she wasn't feeling all that well."

"Don't worry about my grandmother."

"Excuse me! Please don't act like this. Now put her on the phone," I demanded.

"Doctors said she needs to rest and doesn't need any stress. Don't call back."

Before he hung up, I asked, "What doctors?"

"She has kidney cancer. Go worry about your own family." And the line went dead.

Kidney cancer? How could she have been diagnosed so quickly with cancer? Is that asshole messing with me? I called a few mutual friends and asked if they could find out what was going on, and after pacing by the phone for a while, one of them called back and gave me the heartbreaking news. Jo had been diagnosed weeks earlier but hadn't wanted to alarm anyone. The last few days, her kidneys had started to shut down. And now Jeff was guarding her from me. He really knew how to push my buttons.

Over the next few days, Jeff and I fought so bad that we had to resort to the police station to help us trade communication, exchange paperwork, and even drop off the kids. We were at each other's throats, literally.

I had lost all my friends who were related to the high-school—now that we were going through with a separation to get a divorce, the coach's wives disowned me. But honestly, I didn't have time to worry about who accepted me.

I left the kids with Rachel and headed to Memphis with determination for a record-setting night of money. Three large events were taking place in Memphis, and that meant that the club would be packed with heavy-pocket men. And since I was still on the hustle, I knew how to work their money out of their pockets and into my clothing without touching a single bill.

I was an hour into my shift when I took a break and ducked into the dressing room to check my phone. I had a missed call. I looked at the screen a couple of times before it registered with me. Scott had called and had left a message. "Hey, Jeanette. Hope you are doing well. I'm in Memphis and wanted to come to see you if you have any time."

Come see me? Here at the club? I asked myself. I hadn't spoken with him since the day I told him in his office that I was getting back with Jeff. Why in the world would he want to see me? I was intrigued and returned his message through a text.

I'm at the club. If you want to come by, I can visit with you. Tell them at the door who you are, and they'll let you in without pay. He must have been looking at his phone given how quick he replied to my message.

Ok, I'll be there in 5 minutes.

Uh! Just happened to be in Memphis? I wonder who he has been talking to? Can you imagine the expressions on the faces of the girls who work for him if they knew he was coming to the club to see me? I went back on the floor and gave a few lap dances before he got there—I figured he was going to take an hour or so away from me working. *Or is he coming for a personal show and lap dance plus more?*

That question was quickly answered when I saw him enter, escorted to a table by one of our topless girls. He was as out of place as if he were a preacher walking in (though FYI, I have danced for a few of them too). Glancing from stage to stage and girl to girl, you would have thought that Dr. Eichhorn from Searcy, Arkansas was going to break his neck. And you should have seen the relief in his eyes when I walked up. "Did you come here to pick up a girl or just for a drink?" I teased him.

"I don't know, are there any good drinks?" He smiled back.

Pretty good. I just grinned. "So, you were just in Memphis?"

"We both know the truth." He confessed right away. "I came to see you."

Wow! "Well, here I am at my real job. And by the fish-out-of-water look, I'd say you haven't visited many clubs?"

He held up one finger. "My first time."

"We'll have to make it a good one then." And for the following hour, we talked. Talked about Jeff and my final separation and the divorce papers that we had filed and how my kids were doing with all the shit I had put them through. It was a breath of fresh air to talk with him. He was going through a divorce that had started three months earlier and had his two daughters living with him.

A good client of mine walked by and gave me his usual head-nod to a reserved table he always sat at. I was kind of glad to see him, since he paid me $1,500 a night to dance for him, but a little apprehensive about what Scott might think.

"I hate to do this, but I really need to work, and that is a client of mine. If you want to meet in the morning for breakfast, I would like that."

"Nah, I'm going to hang around and have a drink. Go ahead, I know you have to work."

I waved one of the girls over to bring Scott a drink, and when I looked back, I saw them talking. He looked perplexed. I later learned that she told him that he couldn't win me over from the club, that it was a prison that we didn't want to be freed from.

I went to my client, and in a seductive move, I gently placed my hand on his neck and spun around, squaring up to him. I looked back, and Scott's eyes were twice their original size. There was no way he was going to be able to handle seeing me hustle my client.

He got up and started out. I excused myself and jogged after him. "Scott?"

He turned with a mournful smile, "I'm sorry, Jeanette, I can't watch you do this. I thought I could but . . . I just can't."

"I'm sorry, but this is what I do."

"You don't have to." He stared into my eyes.

What the fuck do you mean I don't have to? This is how I make my money! I am Jeanette, and I don't get told what to do! Then, and I can't write this well enough to truly explain, I had an out-of-body experience. I wasn't looking into the eyes of a man I had gone out with a few times. I was staring into the brown eyes of a Peruvian man. His dark-complexed skin, his jet-black hair, and a smile that would melt me where I stood.

Then Scott came back into focus, with his arm extended. "Please, let me take you out of here." I stared at his hand.

Looking back, I had fought this type of chivalry many times through many different relationships. It is so difficult to give up control, especially when you have never been able to trust anyone in the past.

Chapter 34

I'm Jeanette, the dirty little girl from North Little Rock, the homeless little girl with a head full of lice, the quiet little girl whom men had their way with, the unwanted little girl who went unnoticed through life. *Why are you reaching for me? For God's sake, do you realize we are at a strip club where I entertain men to fulfill their sick fantasies?*

His hand never moved, his eyes never blinked, his expression never changed—he wanted me. I took his hand.

To this day, I remember changing to normal clothes and walking out into the night air of Memphis with a feeling of freedom and an untamed emotion of peace. Jeanette, the girl no one would have ever thought, got her knight in shining armor and her Prince Charming, named Scott Eichhorn.

No one in my life had ever said they didn't want me to dance, and I didn't know until it happened that I was longing for affirmation and for someone to rescue me. It's been fourteen years since I left the club, not once going back. I miss the thrill, my friends, and the feeling of having a shit-ton of money, but the love that one man has shown me has trumped all monetary value. Has it been easy? HA! The story isn't over yet.

Funny how things work out—three months after I left the club, they closed their doors. The night I left, Scott walked me to my car, and we followed each other home two hours west to Searcy. We talked all the way home on our cell phones, only losing each other in Wynn Arkansas, a dead spot. Our conversation was platonic and meaningless in its direct words, but powerful in forming a relationship I didn't expect. Peeling off from each other as we reached the city limits of Searcy, we promised to pick back up in the morning over breakfast.

I walked into my house to find Rachel still cuddled up on the couch, deep into a romantic comedy. She was surprised to see me but happy that I was home. We curled up under a warm blanket on the couch and laughed through the remaining movie. As the credits were rolling, we talked about what had happened and how I was done with dancing. I was coming home to be a normal single mother and sell real estate.

We talked throughout the night like sisters, laughing and giggling about silly, pointless things. As the sun touched the sky the next morning, I woke up thinking about breakfast with Scott. I passed by my closet, intending to climb in the shower, but something stopped me. I pulled myself back into the doorway of my closet and looked at the outfits I wore to the club, neatly arranged on one side of the closet. "Not anymore," I said out loud and proceeded to take them down and place them in a pile in the middle of our backyard.

"What are you doing, Mommy?" Amber asked, looking out the back door. The sweet, soft sound of her voice affirmed my actions.

"I am purging life."

"What?" She cocked her head.

"I'm starting a new life baby."

"What are you doing with your clothes?" Dustin joined the conversation.

"You go back to watching your show. I'll fix you something to eat." I didn't want to seem dramatic in front of my kids. Fifteen minutes later, I stood in my kitchen, fixing pop tarts and toast, watching the flames in the pile of my dancer's clothes can grow taller and taller, expelling years of hard work and imprisonment. The gray and blue smoke resembled dark angels being released from their captivity seeking their next prey. Ok, maybe I'm being a little overdramatic, but seeing my clothes burn (expensive clothes I have to add), gave me a sense of peace I cannot explain.

The following Monday, after a few conversations with friends, co-workers, and family members about how I was done with dancing, I was once again the talk of the town. Or so it felt. Scott and I weren't ready to announce that we were seeing each other, and so for a few months, we snuck around, avoiding talk and confrontation from Jeff.

One time, we decided to go to Mexico but not tell anyone that we were traveling together. We were so paranoid that we didn't even walk together at the Little Rock airport. We look back and laugh at the extensive measures we took not to be caught by our friends, our family, and especially Jeff. Scott wasn't scared of Jeff and wanted to confront him on a few occasions, but I asked that he remain quiet, until Mexico.

We were in our room and just happened to have Scott's cell phone on when it rang from a number he didn't recognize from home. It was a number I knew. "Hello?" he answered before I could stop him. "Ah. Hello, Jeff." Scott looked at me with a shit-eating grin.

"I want to stay professional and somewhat adult about this. There's a rumor that you are seeing Jeanette?" I could hear Jeff over the speakerphone.

"Go on."

"I'm not sure if it's true, but I want to ask you to stay away from her."

"It's true, I am seeing Jeanette. I respect you calling in a mature manner, but I am too far into dating Jeanette and I have no intentions on breaking it off."

"Fine. Just watch yourself around town," Jeff warned him.

"Jeff, I'm a dentist in Searcy. I have three children and I am not going to create any more drama. Jeanette is where she wants to be. That's her choice to make and I am not going to have a schoolyard fight with you. Come near me or Jeanette and I will see that you spend time in jail. Clear?"

Jeff hung up, knowing Scott was someone he didn't want to mess with, and he never did.

We spent our vacation enjoying each other and thinking about how we were going to break the news of our relationship to our friends and family back home. We knew everyone would be fine with it except his assistants at the clinic. To be honest, I was nervous about meeting them for the first time as Scott's girlfriend. We flew home and made the announcement.

Chapter 35

Through my family, the vibe was the same—the kids liked the idea of Scott being a new guy, but they did miss Jeff being there day in and day out. Rachel was happy that we made it official because she was the only one outside of Scott and me who knew. The girls at the clinic had a million questions for Scott and none for me when I showed up not as a patient. But I knew in time that would fade away, and we would become close.

I tried calling Jo, but Jeff guarded that phone very closely and wouldn't let me speak to her. I was so angry at him—how could he keep me from talking to her? I had thought about just going over to her house, but I didn't want the stress of Jeff and I fighting to hurt her, physically or mentally.

Scott's parents were a different situation. They were pleasant and very welcoming when I met them for the first time, but I could tell his mother had her reserves. Later, I learned through Scott that she had been praying that he and his ex-wife would reconcile. Scott had explained my story to his parents, and I don't think it resulted in any judgment toward me. If fact, his mother and I were extremely similar in many ways.

It was a Friday morning and I had just sat down at my desk in my office when my cell buzzed with a call. I turned it over to see it was Jeff. It was the day our divorce was final, but I wasn't sure why he was calling. *Does he want to back out of the divorce? Does he want to celebrate? Should I even answer?*

I picked up the phone. "Hey, Jeff."

"Jo's dying," he said in a somber voice.

At first, I wanted to say no shit, she has cancer, but him calling meant something. "What's going on?" I asked.

"You need to head over if you want to see her before she passes."

Time stopped. My heart stopped. A call that I never thought I would get—a woman I'd thought would outlive us all. I told him I'd be right over and hung up in a daze. I called Scott and told him that I was going to her house. I don't remember the drive there, I don't remember if I talked to anyone else, and I'm not sure what I was thinking as I drove but walking up to the front door, I had an uneasy feeling sweep over me.

Jeff opened the door, and with the sun shining on his face I could see the tears filling his eyes. He didn't say anything, he just wrapped his arms around me and began crying, as if he had been holding it back until I got there. I hugged him back. "Has she passed?" I squeaked out.

"No," he answered with his head buried in my shoulder.

We talked for a moment and then I went into the house where I found other friends, family, and Valley Baptist's pastor. Jeff's parents had recently moved to Cabot, Arkansas, and they were sitting on the couch when I walked in. Jeff's mother stood and hugged me, asking how I had been. It was just small talk; I believe she knew the story with Scott and myself.

She took me by my hand and guided me back to Jo's room. She pushed open the door to a frail and pale-skinned woman I barely recognized. Jo was resting on her bed, unaware of her surroundings. "I'll give you some time," Jeff's mother told me and backed out of the room.

I looked around the room—everything looked the same with the exception of the oxygen tank beside the bed and a few other pieces of medical equipment. I knelt down beside her bed and took her hand. It was warm but thin, with very little muscle tone. I started to speak, but nothing but tears came out.

They say that when someone dies, you go through five stages of grieving. I believe I went through all five stages in a matter of minutes. At first, I denied that this was even happening, not to a woman who had treated me as her own. I was so angry that I hadn't forced my way over to see her while she was still in decent health. I bargained with God, then slumped down in self-pity. The acceptance part, well, I went through four of the five. I still haven't come to accept the truth yet.

I pulled myself back up to her side. "Jo?" I asked in a soft voice. "I hope you can hear me. It's Jeanette. I've missed you." I took a deep breath. "I haven't been fair to you at all. I should have forced my way over here to see you, but I was afraid of what Jeff would have done. Probably nothing."

I felt my heart began to beat faster as the words began coming to my mouth and to Jo's ears. "I will always be grateful for the encouragement and positive influence you were in my life. Thank you for being the greatest grandmother I could have ever asked for to my children. I know people have guardian angels . . . would you please be mine?"

And as if she had waited on me to see her, I watched her chest rise, and with a gasp of air, I saw it lower as she exhaled her last breath. Emotions poured over me, and in a desperate cry, I shouted, "Please don't leave, Jo! Please stay with us." I paused for—I'm not sure how long. "Go home Jo, go home." I let go of her hand.

Jeff's mother's hand gently landed on my shoulder. "She knows sweetheart, she knows."

I met Jeff in the living room, and again he broke down, embracing me. "I've now lost two of the most important women in my life." With all the turmoil and strife we'd been through, and all the disagreements and fights, I figured I would have laughed at his statement, but instead my heart broke for him too.

Chapter 36

I have been through many losses in my life, and I have lived through a lot of shit, but losing Jo hit me harder than anything I had gone through. She had been in my life for a short ten years but looking back at the wisdom she shared with me, I know that I learned more from her than from anyone else in my life. My grandmother was a great person and dearly loved me, but her love only went so far, with the many family members that drained her affection like a flock of vampires.

I slowly drove home with mixed emotions, in deep thought about the past 29 years of my life. I can truly say that I have been through valleys and have seen the summits of mountains, but I questioned myself if I had had that true mountaintop experience. Adversity is something that I knew I had overcome in more ways than most people have had to deal with, and I knew that life was going great. I had healthy children, a great job, a nice house and car (paid for), and a wonderful and successful boyfriend. But for some reason, I was missing something, and I could not put my finger on it. I blew it off, blaming emotions.

The funeral was planned for the following day at Valley Baptist Church, a building I hadn't been in since I broke out crying during one of their songs. I was hoping they wouldn't remember me. Scott had decided that it might be best that he not attend, with there being a negative relationship with Jeff and his family.

I was close to being ready when my phone rang with a call from Jeff. "Hey, Jeff."

"Should I wear a red tie or blue?" he asked in a helpless tone.

"You should wear the blue one. Do you still have the dark blue one with the square designs on it?"

"Yeah, I'm holding it."

"Wear that one." I paused. "Are you ok?"

"No."

Thinking it through for only a short moment, I asked, "Do I need to come and get you?"

"I really don't want to drive alone. Do you mind?"

"I'll be there in twenty minutes." I hung up the phone and shot Scott a quick text that I was driving Jeff. Before I could get out of the house, he replied, questioning if that was a good idea. I assured him I knew what was best and I was only driving him. I would call when we got out.

We pulled up to the half-filled parking lot of the church, watching a few elderly people filing in to find their seats. Jeff and I stepped out to a warm, welcoming smile from the pastor and a couple of members of the church. Walking in, I drifted back to the day when I went with Jo to a Sunday service, and she introduced me to everyone who was there. She was so happy that I had gone with her, though I expect she was excited that anyone of us went with her.

The wooden pews were filled with ladies dressed in black dresses and men in dark suits, each one of them acknowledging our entrance and giving us a nod of gratitude. I sat up front with Jeff and his family during the service and listened to the preacher talk about the legacy Jo had left behind. I was taken aback a little, not realizing she had given so much time, service and money to what she believed in or was led by God to be involved in. Wow, big shoes to fill for any of us.

The procession wasn't long, but it was filled with dear friends and beloved family members. Jo was laid to rest on the west side of town in a small cemetery that she had picked out. Big wreaths and large flower arrangements circled the mahogany casket with the backdrop of blue skies and a sparse cloud occasionally floating by.

The preacher said a couple of short words then dismissed the family with a short prayer. I hugged Jeff's family goodbye, thinking this was one of the last times that I would see them, though that proved to be different in time. I texted Scott and let him know that it was over, but I needed to go home and get some sleep. He replied that he would check in with me the next day.

A steaming-hot shower and a warm bed were what I was longing for after a day of shedding tears and trying to keep some composure. Normally I go to sleep with the TV on and set the timer for an hour for it to shut off, but that night I didn't remember my head hitting the pillow. I woke up to beating rays of sun shining on my face with the window blinds aimed down. *Holy shit, where did the night go?*

My phone buzzed with a text, keeping me from going back to sleep. *Damn it! This had better be a client who wants to sell a million-dollar house.* I looked at my phone to see it was Jeff, asking if he could come over. *Shit!*

Give me a little time. I texted back.

That little time was all of fifteen minutes. I could hear Jeff's truck coming down the road with his tires roaring on the pavement, and shortly after there was a knock at the door. We had not been sitting at the kitchen table for even five minutes when Scott called. *What great timing.* I signaled to Jeff that I'd be right back, but he knew who was on the phone and followed me into the living room.

"Hey Scott," I answered, and before he could say anything back, Jeff asked who I was talking to.

"Is Jeff there?" Scott asked without saying hello.

"Yes," I confessed.

"This early? Wait, did he spend the night?"

"No! He just came over." I tried to talk with him, but Jeff started making a scene. "This isn't a good time. Call me later." I made a gesture at Jeff to leave.

"Call you later?" Scott asked over the phone, confused.

"No, not you. I was asking Jeff to leave."

"I'm on my way over." Scott hung up.

I looked at Jeff. "I know a lot has happened lately, but now isn't a good time." I walked Jeff to the door and let him out.

Moments later, Scott was knocking on my door, and my first thought was *holy shit, I don't need this today*. I let him in.

"Are you and Jeff getting back together?" he questioned me.

"What the fuck?" I snapped. I knew through multiple conversations with Scott that he'd never suffered a close loss and didn't understand the emotions that were bleeding through Jeff's family.

"I can't do this," he said.

"Can't do what?" I answered. "I only took Jeff to the funeral, and I am not sure why he came here this morning, but

I told him to leave. I am the one who can't do this right now. I haven't had any time to grieve!"

He looked at me, and with a gentle voice said, "You want to go fishing?"

Chapter 37

My first thought was, *you want to take me where*? The old-school Jeanette wanted to ask what the fuck was he thinking, fishing? This new Jeanette thought for a bit and finally spoke. "Sure, take me fishing."

To this day, I am not sure if he had planned on us going fishing, but he had three fishing rods and a tackle box in his truck when I walked outside with him. He had decided to take me to a small-town west of Searcy called Heber Springs, which was the home of the Greers Ferry Lake and the world-class trout-fishing river, the Little Red River. It was a short drive over, and within half an hour we were at a resort with a large dock filled with small metal boats, each with a twenty-five-horsepower outboard motor.

Thank God I brought a jacket—the water was a whopping 43 degrees, refrigerating the air above it to an icy feel. He paid the front desk for a day's rental, a Styrofoam can of bait, three sticks of beef jerky, and a bag of mini-marshmallows. I had heard of binge snacking and had participated in my share, but jerky and marshmallows were a little over the top. I learned later that the trout love mini marshmallows and Scott loves beef jerky.

He really didn't say anything or ask many questions while we fished, just simple ones about being outdoors. The sun had reached its peak, pushing down the heat that April was known to produce here at times. The blast of the horn from the dam a couple of miles upriver signaled that it was about to open and allow a larger amount of water into the river, something that Scott didn't seem too concerned about.

The current picked up, pushing floating leaves past us, and taking the small boat farther downstream into a thick fog caused by the temperature change. Scott reeled in a few small fish while I drifted off in the sun, fighting to break through too much-needed rest. Have you ever been stuck between sleep and wake but felt totally at rest? That was where I was.

I drifted back to my childhood and to the visions of my father bringing me gifts to the small wood-framed house where we lived in North Little Rock. He wasn't a big man in stature, but in the eyes of a five-year-old girl, he was the king of all men. His skin would shine in the sunlight, and in my mind, I could see him flipping his black locks out of his face with one jerk of his head. My mother would sit with me on the front porch, and together we'd listen to the stories of Peru that my father would tell. It was good to reflect back to the positive memories that happened in my life; it was some strange effect that Scott had on my mind.

"You going to reel that one in?" He pulled me out of my sleep.

"Oh shit!" I yelled, looking at my rod bent over with a fish on the end of it. He just laughed as I struggled to grab the rod before it dove over the side of the boat. I reeled it in and swung the fish over to Scott. "Do you mind? I don't want to smell like fish." I smiled.

"And you came fishing why?" he answered.

"Oh, I don't know. Maybe because you kidnapped me," I replied with a smirk.

Time seemed to stand still on the water, and if I could've had any control over it, I wouldn't have let it move at all. I admired the fact that Scott was good at doing what needed to be done, getting me out of my norm. It's a skill he hasn't lost. He is so damn good at giving me space but suffocating me with love at the same time. *How in the hell does he do it?*

And for the first time in my life, I finally got why men love to go fishing, play golf, go camping, and do other mindless activities. It's simple—it takes their mind off the stress of day-to-day life. I learned on that day of fishing that I need mindless days in my life, and I can truly admit that this realization has helped shape me into the woman I am today.

I'm not an uber-bible-beating Christian, but I get why God put in the Ten Commandments to keep the Sabbath Day holy. It's not about the church and all the other people, it's about us resting our bodies, minds, and souls. And if you're into God, it's about being in His presence. That's it—nothing hard about it.

Scott showed me more than just fishing that day. He showed me how to escape from life and keep my sanity. He gave me peace that day. Peace I needed. Something I really had never experienced before. I will always be thankful to him for that, and it's something I hope I can pass down to my grandkids.

Chapter 38

The following weeks were like something out of a romance story—well, maybe more like a romantic comedy. Scott's parents took me in like I was one of the family, and his sisters loved sharing stories that embarrassed him. For the first time I was in a stable relationship, and Scott would say little things that were uplifting and encouraging. This was something foreign to me. At times, I would play scenarios in my head of us getting in a fight and how I would defend myself if it happened, but soon those thoughts faded as we didn't fight like in my past relationships.

We planned a trip to Florida to see my stepmother, someone whom I had tried to keep close with but living fourteen hours apart that relationship was primarily through the phone. Scott suggested we invite the entire family down, and once we got everyone there, the party was on. The second night, we went salsa dancing, and with drinks flowing and the excitement in the air, we managed to close the place down then head to a Cuban restaurant that was open twenty-four hours. They loved the Arkansas crowd—loud and Southern!

The following night was New Year's, and the party started early but never left my stepmother's house. Both sides of the family got along great, giving Scott and I much-needed peace with our recent splits.

What I didn't expect happened while everyone was dancing in my stepmother's living room. Scott faced me and then dropped to one knee. "You son-of-a-bitch, this is why you invited everyone!" And in front of my family and his, he asked for my hand in marriage. I said, "Hell yes!"

My Prince Charming had arrived.

Jeff had started seeing someone else, and before Scott and I knew about it, he had married her. It lifted many stressful situations off our shoulders, and after a short time, Jeff became civil in our meetings; the words written in this book cannot describe the change we saw in our kids; a beautiful change.

The wedding was planned for June, and we all flew to St. Petersburg, Florida to marry on the white sandy beaches of the Gulf of Mexico. The resort was more than accommodating to both sides of the family, and on several occasions helped organize the massive amount of people we brought with us.

We had t-shirts made that read "The Eichhorn Family and Wedding." It was a gift that I thought our family would stick in their luggage. Nope, not this family. They wore their shirts tall and proud. I even believe a few of them wore them too much without washing them.

I know that throughout this book, I have explained how my mother was absent many times throughout my life, but not for this wedding. Part of me wanted to blame the reason for her coming on the elaborate accommodations, but she made a comment to me while taking a picture with Scott and me. "You are so beautiful, and you and Scott make a great couple. This is the man that you are to spend the rest of your life with!"

Wow! I was speechless and just smiled for the camera. Here stood my mother, not perfect, scarred from battling her demons, but as supportive as I have ever seen her. It set the stage for the perfect wedding I had dreamed about for many years.

Fun fact, though—my mother had never flown before, and somehow, she missed her connecting flight, making her late to the ceremony. I wasn't upset, and her eyes told me all I needed to know. She wanted to be there more than anyone.

But there was one person missing who had been a role model to me ever since she took me in at a young age. My grandmother. Over the last year, she had gone down quickly with Alzheimer's, and though she was still living at home, there were many days she was confused and clueless. She had shared with me many times that when I ever felt alone, she'd always be there in spirit, and during the ceremony, I felt her presence.

Most of my family that was there was my Hispanic side (Dad's family), and they were so different than Scott's family, but everyone meshed. And loading the buses to make a family trip to Busch Gardens was more entertaining than the tour of the gardens itself. Thirty-five-plus people all carrying on their own conversations and ignoring Scott, me, the bus driver, the tour guide, the waitress at the restaurant, and anyone else who wanted to get their two cents in.

The second evening there, the family dressed in khaki and white and made their way out to a sugar-white, sandy beach. Scott and I wore black and white, not for any symbolic reason, just to stand out from the rest of the family.

God showed up at my first wedding as a grumpy old justice of the peace; he showed up at my second wedding as a destructive tornado; and now, God showed up at my third wedding in fashionista style. During the ceremony, the sky erupted in fire. In the distance, we could see an explosion on the horizon that only our creator could make. He had placed long, grayish clouds that exemplified the definition of a silver lining, and on the edge of the ocean, he placed the most remarkable sunset you could ever imagine.

The minister announced us as husband and wife and instructed Scott to kiss his bride, me! And to this day that kiss has never left my lips. The family clapped and cheered, then broke off to the buffet that waited. Scott and I and our immediate family stayed behind for pictures. It was the first time that I realized how big our family was going to be, and how great the years to come.

This was the start of the rest of my life. The start to something precious that God had given not only me but also my children. We spent a couple more days enjoying family and kids, and there were a lot of kids. We sent them home to Arkansas, and Scott and I flew from Florida to Antigua for our honeymoon. A solid seven days of nothing but lounging on the beach and enjoying each other.

This was it, and this would be a great place to wrap up my story. But again, I'm not that simple, and my story with my Prince Charming and his white horse doesn't end here.

Chapter 39

Five weeks after our honeymoon, Ashton was turning three, and I have to admit that I am one of those crazy birthday-party mothers, so I threw one hell of a party. Both sides of the family came, along with Jeff and his new wife. We rented a couple of bounce houses and decorated the inside of the house and the out. This is where I think my Peruvian inheritance shines through—go big or go home when throwing a birthday party.

Kids were everywhere, grandparents were trying to take pictures, moms were bragging about their children, and dads were comparing lawnmowers. Just your typical Southern birthday party.

I was in the kitchen removing the cake from the box it had been delivered in when Jeff walked in. "You've done a good job throwing this party," he said. *Wait! Did my ex just compliment me? Did it take dragging me through hell and a messy divorce to finally get a compliment out of him?*

"Thank you, the kids have said they like your new wife."

"Yea, she is pretty cool. I'm happy that we are able to be social, you know, Scott and myself."

I just shook my head in agreement, thinking that it wasn't Scott who was being hard to get along with. One trait of many that Scott has is patience. "Grab those paper plates." I motioned to a stack on the countertop. Rachel walked in and helped carry out a few things.

"I remember the parties we had for Dustin and Amber. Those were good times," he replied.

I smiled. "They were, Jeff. And we can still have good times at their future parties." I am not sure what he picked up from me saying that, but he patted my shoulder. *SHIT! I'm not supposed to feel those vibes anymore.* I quickly shook them off and dashed out the door, yelling for everyone to gather around and sing Happy Birthday.

Scott slid up beside me. "Everything ok?" He nodded toward Jeff.

"Yes, for the first time in a long time our conversation was calm."

"Good. Hopefully, all that is past us," Scott responded before busting into the lead of singing Happy Birthday.

The days to follow were simple and routine, with the small exception that Jeff started texting me. It started with a "thank you for inviting us to the party" and then led into funny emails that were innocent. And of course, that led to casual conversations about the past and the good times we had shared.

I was reading one of those emails when Scott walked into the kitchen and caught a glimpse. "What are you doing?" He asked.

"Oh, Jeff sent a message."

"About?"

"Nothing in general."

"If it's not about the kids, then you two have nothing to discuss."

I looked up from the screen. "Excuse me?"

"It's not healthy or fair to me that you are talking with your ex-husband."

I closed down the screen and stood up. "Don't preach to me, and don't you dare try to tell me what to do!" I walked out, pissed as hell.

A couple of days passed, and everything was fine between Scott and myself. I know I had been flirting with danger keeping the conversation between Jeff and me going, and I had decided to end it. We had a lot of history, a lot of history that was filled with weird toxicity that was hard to shake.

My cell phone rang, and I looked down to see Jeff calling. "Hello," I answered.

"Let's make this work."

I wanted to play it off and ask what he was talking about, but I knew before he called. "Jeff, we have started different lives with different people." I quietly prayed that he'd agree and hang up.

"I don't care. You and I have too much to give up. Come home!"

Timing is everything, right? Not for me. I was having this conversation while Scott's youngest daughter was having her senior pictures taken. I was the one who had taken her. "Ok," I said to Jeff and explained that I needed to call Scott.

I hung up with Jeff. It makes me sick to my stomach to even write this part, but I called Scott. I explained that I hadn't lost my feelings for Jeff and I was going to go back to him. All the men I had been around in my life would have screamed and cussed and thrown shit in the background while telling me what to do. Not Scott.

"I don't think you are thinking this through. Let's spend a couple of days to talk this through," he replied.

That should have been a slap in my face, but I was on this one-way path of a love high that had blinded me and made me ignorant to the truth. "I'm sorry, Scott. I'm going back."

There was a long pause on the phone. "Fine. You have to tell my daughter what you are doing. You know she worships the ground you walk on. Don't lead her to believe that you are in the right." He hung up.

I dropped my head down. "Fuck!" That was one conversation I didn't ever want to have.

Minutes later, she pounced into the car, "Those were the best pictures ever, what do you think?" she asked me. I had watched most of her pictures before Jeff had called.

"I have to tell you something," I replied, with tears in my eyes.

Teenagers are smarter than we give them credit for. She studied me for a short time. "You're leaving my father."

"This isn't a decision I just made. It's something I have no control over," I tried to explain.

"Whatever you have done he will forgive you. He loves you! We love you, don't do this!" she begged.

In all my life, I was never led to drugs or even entertaining that lifestyle, but I believe I can understand the addiction part. Love has got to be the strongest drug ever invented. The only problem is that many people are led down a path they believe is love when it's only the motions and not the intimacy. This was the path I was on with Jeff. Love in relationships can only exist in a dual manner. Each person has to truly love each other in the agape love that is stronger than any feeling a human can generate. Relationships with a one-way love path are set for one thing: failure.

Chapter 40

I am assuming that 90 percent of my readers right now either hate me or think I am the biggest dumbass in the world. At this point in my story, I would go with the hate me. My life hasn't been a basket of sunshine or easy by any means. I came from pretty much nothing. By the world's standards and statistics, I should be on welfare living off the government, in prison, or dead.

But this is what my earthly savior taught me.

Jeff and I lasted almost three months before I realized what I was doing. He had slipped back to his normal ways, and our fighting flared back up where it had left off a year earlier. I threw his shit out in the front yard and told him to get out and never to call again. After heated words, he loaded his truck and drove away.

I marched into the house with temper flaring, not thinking straight. Then it hit me like a professional boxer might land their best punch on a little five-foot-three, dark brown-haired girl. I fell to the ground in an uncontrollable emotion that I had never experienced. With my back leaning on the laundry room door, I cried as I had never cried before. Not for what I had just gone through, but for what I had given up months earlier.

I had found love in a person that I had never expected. I had found that once in a lifetime, agape love that so many people search for their whole lives, and I had given it up. For what? And why? I had beaten so many difficult experiences and circumstances, just to give it all up for a one-way path of self-destruction.

I spent the following days in a self-pity depression and fell into such a self-esteem problem that I moved out of Searcy and went back to Vilonia. I know my kids and Rachel were dragged through hell and back and sitting at my kitchen table just down the road from where I grew up, I made a decision. I wasn't going to lose! My father was a warrior to his last living breath, and I was going to continue his legacy by picking myself up and making something out of myself.

This is something hard to do when you have the demon of depression shoving a double-edged sword through your heart. Over the next couple of months, I battled every day to make it in the business world, love my kids, and keep my sanity. I was fighting, praying to my father for help, and trying to do everything myself.

Then, on a self-pity night, he called.

The bible speaks of five different types of angels. I believe they left out the sixth and most important angel God could ever send. Our Earthly angel.

"You ok?" Scott asked on the other end of the line.

"Why are you calling me?"

"You need someone," he answered.

How in the hell do you know that? I thought. I stayed quiet.

"How are the kids?" he asked.

"They are…" I paused, wondering if I should tell him the truth. Then I answered, "They're not doing good." I was honest.

"Me neither. I'll be truthful, I've been battling some pretty serious depression."

Have you ever tried taking a deep breath and break out into tears at the same time? I couldn't answer. I wanted to, but I couldn't speak.

"Come home, Jeanette. I need you."

Chapter 41

I was standing in front of my living room window in Vilonia, Arkansas trying to comprehend what had taken place in my life. Not just in the last year, but in the last twenty years, which had passed by like a dream. I had made bad decisions in my life and the previous night on the phone with someone who was trying to rescue me, I made a decision that would bring me to where I am now. I was a fighter! I didn't need anyone to help me; I could do it by myself.

"Mommy?" Amber gripped my hand.

"Yes, sweetie?"

"Christmas is coming, is Santa going to stop by our place this year?" she asked in that sweet little innocent voice.

"Yes, sweetheart. Santa is coming this year. And every year for the rest of your life." I smiled.

Dustin tightened my other hand. "Mom!" He stared out the window.

"I see him," I replied, watching the four-door tan truck pull into our drive with Scott behind the wheel. "We're going home." I tried to wipe the tears falling down my face.

Fighters are trained. The trait comes naturally, but without learning how to harness its power and control, a fighter goes into battle blind. My savior, my trainer, the last man I have ever loved, pulled into my driveway that day. Not to only take me home but to give my kids and Rachel a home that is warm, safe, and full of love.

I opened the door for Scott to enter, and before he grabbed a bag or packed a box, he grabbed me. I'd been hugged many times by my father. Hugs that expressed all the emotions of love that I never thought I would ever experience again after his death. With Scott's arms wrapped around me, I had an out-of-body experience that I can only explain with a heavenly term agape.

We loaded his truck, the kids found their seats well before everything was packed, and we started our trek back to Searcy. A town where I had been big news, then forgotten about, then talked about, prayed for, and accepted.

But my day wasn't over—actually, my day hadn't even begun. We were heading home for me to face Scott's kids, a group that I had abandoned five months earlier. They knew I was coming, and two of the three were waiting on us at the door. They welcomed Rachel and my kids back and gave me a look I didn't deserve. A look that was warm and forgiving. Not Scott's oldest daughter, though.

He brought her into the living-room where I sat with my children much like a defendant would sit during a trial. It wasn't really set up this way, just something in my imagination.

"Why are you letting her come back?" she asked her father while shooting daggers through me with her eyes.

"I love Jeanette through thick and thin. She is coming home, and I need you to understand."

"Not a cold day in hell!"

Scott's oldest son piped up. "Dad loves her. It's not your decision if she comes home. It's your decision if you are going to crucify her in front of Dad!"

Silence swept the room. I watched her take a deep breath, and though I wasn't worthy, we locked eyes. "He is my everything," she said.

"And I will never hurt him. I am promising you," I replied.

I'm not sure what it feels like to have the Holy Spirit fill the room, but that night had to have been close. Scott's youngest took a deep breath and gave me something I didn't deserve; forgiveness.

His hand tightened around mine. His family, in one sitting, had forgiven me for my abandonment and given me the greatest gift of all. And then, as if nothing had ever happened, she turned to her father. "Christmas is just a couple of days away. What are we going to get the kids?" She was referring to my three.

I was taught by Scott's daughter that night that forgiveness is being loved when you can't be loved anymore.

The following day, Scott's mother and father came over to meet with me. It was an emotional day that I wasn't expecting. Scott's mother is much like me—strong-willed, speaks her mind, and controls the room. She cried. *No! You aren't supposed to cry; you're supposed to cuss me out and tell me how sorry I am.*

Scott's father, business-oriented and direct, showed me compassion greater than that of any other man alive.

My entire life was wrecked in twelve hours. These people were supposed to hate me, throw stones, cuss me out, beat me. Why? Why are they forgiving me?

Chapter 42

Christmas came quicker than I can remember and along with the holiday of the birth of the savior came much anxiety. Days earlier I had been given the ultimate gift of forgiveness and now I was celebrating the holiday in honor of the person who gave us forgiveness. I was truly freaking out over the entire day, and all over the main event: dinner. Scott's entire family had made plans to be there and all I could think about was them asking, "Why did you let Jeanette back in?"

But to my relief and astonishment, no one brought up the subject and they treated me and my kids as if we had never left. I sat across from Scott's father and listened to him entertain the family with stories from their past, laughing about the good times. Something I secretly couldn't wait to be part of, the good times! Our kids got along great and

Scott's kids loved having us back in their lives and loved sharing their family and home with us.

Over the following year, things were perfect. My kids had transferred back to Searcy schools and found their old friends who welcomed them back just like Scott's kids. I stayed at home getting the six kids off to school and taking care of the house while Scott worked. It had become my safe place. In the early afternoons with a silent house, I was able to sit on our leather sofa and breath with no worries.

With freedom and time to myself came boredom. I was madly in love with Scott and he fulfilled my every need for affection and companionship, but I started missing self-purpose in my life. I sat down with him one evening and asked what he thought about me going to cosmetology school.

"Sounds great. When and where were you thinking?" was his answer.

"It's local and I would start right away. My cousin could move in and help with the kids. Like a nanny," I answered.

He smiled, "I think it's a great idea."

And so did I. I had spent so much time trying to sell beautiful that it made sense to help others find their beauty whether it be through make-up or hairstyles. The following year I finished cosmetology school and started working at a nearby salon. I met lots of people and made many great friends. I worked part-time so I could spend as much time with my family as I could.

I had waited tables, danced on stage, worked at a bank, sold real estate, and now worked at a salon, but I was still not content. Something was missing and I couldn't figure it out. Scott and I sat down once again and talked about it. "Jeanette, you've always been a person who was in charge. Somehow we need to figure out how to fuel that dominate gene you have."

It was as if a light turned on in my head. "What would you think about me opening my own business?" I asked.

"What kind of business?"

I couldn't answer him just yet. Over the following weeks, I did my research to find what aspect of cosmetology was missing in our area. I found it.

I called Scott, "I want to open a wax center."

Without hesitation, "That sounds pretty cool. Let's do it!"

And so, we started the process of opening my own business. It was much harder than I had expected and tested every bit of my patience. I had mostly worked for other people and hadn't learned the ethics of being a business owner. I contacted the European Wax Center in the interest of placing one of their franchise in Searcy. They replied to set up a conference call. *What?* I had never been on a conference call, come to think of it I had never sat in a conference meeting.

I was so nervous on the phone that I couldn't answer simple questions. But somehow through my fumbling of words and sounds of inexperience, they agreed to partner with me. "Sweet! I have found multiple sites here in Searcy and I believe…"

"Jeanette, Jeanette. Slow down. We aren't interested in Searcy. We want to be in Little Rock," they replied.

"But I live in Searcy."

"Little Rock is the bigger market."

After our call, I went to find Scott and asked what he thought of Little Rock. Scott had played the biggest role in helping me open my business, he was my coach, cheerleader, and greatest supporter. "Jeanette, there is no doubt in my mind that you already know where the best place is."

A smile formed across my face and I became a business owner.

After careful considerations of many different locations, I opened my first European Wax Center in North Little Rock. In the neighborhood where it all had started. I had managed to come full circle in my life and to return as a champion. The wax center was located across the street from the school where I was abused, tormented, and embarrassed.

I walked out my door many times and stared at the school that was a symbol of my defeat in my earlier years. Now it was a symbol of me giving back to a community that had taken so much. I hired 15 amazing women and together we revealed beautiful skin and gave women confidence in their daily lives.

Now, fast forward to 2019. I own three European Wax Centers and employ over 50 women. I couldn't have done this without the support of my family. They say it takes a village and I couldn't agree more. In a village, you have many different people who play vital roles in seeing the success of a villager. In my village, I had the cheerleaders, the pushers, the coach, the moral supporters, and most of all the forgivers.

Chapter 43

There isn't a day that goes by that I don't ask myself how I got here. Among all the shit that came my way, I have been able to battle through what life dealt me. This wasn't a learned trait; I believe I inherited it through my father. Looking back, I wouldn't change a thing because the past has made me look forward to the future.

As a business owner with over fifty women on staff, I have been asked many times what drives my leadership. It isn't an easy question to answer and too many it's a surprising answer. I've sat in many workshops, conferences, leadership training, and one-on-one coaching, all of which have different ideas for being a successful business owner.

What drives my leadership? Forgiveness.

It was a gift that I had blindly been offered many times in my life but it wasn't until Scott's daughter gave me that precious gift of forgiveness that I understand the power of it. I didn't hone that power until I started forgiving others. I also believe that forgiveness has molded me into the wife, mother, and business owner I am today.

But... it wasn't as easy as I make it sound. There were many questions that I had to muddle through and answers that didn't come overnight. And to become completely forgiving I had to fight the one person that I feared the most, the one person that could whip me with one punch, the person I had lied to so many times... me.

I am the type of person that if I am going to work on something, I have to understand the meaning and the framework of that subject. One of the first questions I had to answer for myself was *"What is the true meaning of forgiveness?"*

I am sure that this could be different for other people. But I was working on me, and/or fighting with me. Looking back at the moment that Scott's daughter forgave me and seeing her precious face I came up with "letting it go." I know it sounds silly but it's part of a complicated answer. Not only do we have to let it go but we have to become completely honest with ourselves to give and receive forgiveness.

The true meaning of forgiveness is letting go of the hate and anger that someone has created and to give them in return compassion and love. That shit isn't easy. Trust me.

I needed to forgive many things and people in my life, people who had hurt me, both physically and mentally. One of the first things I forgave was my parenting. I had pointed a finger at my mom for so long that I didn't realize the damage I was inflicting on my own children. Hell, I dragged them all over the country and almost killed them in a car wreck. The more I realized it the more I grew angry with myself. But I had to let that go and forgive myself.

I had to forgive my thoughts. My thoughts had become so tainted with hate and negativity I didn't realize the effect they had on others. And because of many of those thoughts, I had to forgive my actions. I told you this shit isn't easy. But once I learned to forgive myself it was so much easier to forgive people who had hurt me.

My mother was easier to forgive than I thought. I was able to see the demons she was battling with and see that we weren't all that much different. I just hope that one day she can face those demons and love herself as much as I love her.

I challenge you to write a list of what you need to forgive, and I would completely understand if that list is over a page long. It is one of the first things we should do to start receiving this powerful gift. And it will make the next list easier to fill out.

Why should we forgive?

Hate, anger, and negativity are the leaders in slavery. When a person is wrapped up in these three emotions, they become enslaved to a world of misery and disappointment. The top reason we should forgive is freedom. I can't explain in words the relief and weight lifted when you can receive the freedom of letting it go and forgiving. Along with freedom comes happiness, joy, self-love, love from others, and love love love love!

Why is forgiveness important?

It's how we grow. It's a seed that we get to plant, cultivate, and watch grow. If you wake up and tell yourself all morning that today is going to be a great day, today is going to be a great day. Guess what? Today is going to be a great day. Forgiving others, whether they want it or not, is planting a seed of love. And what happens to a seed if you don't take care of it? It dies. Cultivating forgiveness is part of the growth and will release you from the slavery of emotions.

Whoever came up with "forgive and forget" doesn't fucking get it. It's hard for me to believe that people live by this rule; how would they learn from something they forgot? I believe that remembering what happened is part of our journey. Instead of pointing at the situation, point at the positives and the wonderful experiences and forget the negatives.

Martin Luther King said, *"Forgiveness does not mean ignoring what has been done or putting a false label on an evil act. It means, rather, that the evil act no longer remains as a barrier to the relationship. Forgiveness is a catalyst creating the atmosphere necessary for a fresh start and a new beginning. It is the lifting of a burden or the canceling of a debt."*

Chapter 44

What do we forgive and <u>why</u> were somewhat easy to answer; it was the <u>when</u> question that was hard for me. I understood the reasons but when it was time for me to step up and act, it was a little more difficult than I thought.

When is the right time to forgive?

For me, I believe that forgiveness didn't truly happen until I was close to 30 years old. Throughout my journey, I had made up a story that justified my lies and my actions. It wasn't until I was forgiven by Scott's family that I understood the true meaning of changing myself for the better and could receive the benefits of forgiveness.

We all have our own journey, trekking down the path I had chosen was my journey. I can use the analogy of sales. You don't ever really sell anyone, you educate them on what the benefits are. The result? You make the sale. Forgiveness is something that is learned and not inherited. Some gain this from family structure, religion, or belief. I had none of these or at least I didn't recognize them until I received it from someone that I had much respect for.

Mark Twain said, *"Forgiveness is the fragrance that the violet sheds on the heel that has crushed it."* Wouldn't it be a miracle if we could all forgive the instant we were hurt or wronged? For some, the Godly people I know, it comes that simple and easy. For me, not so! I am working on it, but I have to be honest and say that finding the right time to forgive has always been a struggle. The older I get the easier it is to forgive quicker. Maybe it's because the older I get the more I am feeling love and joy from forgiveness. Or maybe it's because of the experiences I have developed over the years.

A note to my younger readers; don't keep yourself enslaved because of someone else's actions. Woman up or man up and go out on that shaking limb and forgive those that have hurt you. Especially yourself.

This leads to another question that is closely related; when in a victim's life does a person realize they can let go of the hurt?

First, do you feel like a victim? If so, what could you change in the course of your story to make you NOT be the victim? I was lured into bed at 16 by a thirty-six-year-old man, an experience that put me in the victim's seat. For me to gain the strength to forgive him I focused on something other than the act. In my case, it was my beautiful son who has given me wonderful experiences that I can't compare to the act.

I AM NOT TELLING YOU TO FORGET! I am telling you to focus on the positive. It sucks! You were raped. I know, it isn't fair. But forgiving the person who did it is winning over them and setting yourself free. And maybe finding something good, in my case something great, that came from the circumstance.

When? Only you know. What I can suggest is make it sooner rather than later.

For years I wanted those who hurt me to feel the same way I felt. Being molested, beaten, embarrassed, and the list could add up, but I STOPPED ADDING. After experiencing the freedom of forgiveness, I wanted more, and my list went from wanting to hurt others to spilling compassion.

"Most of us need time to work through pain and loss. We can find all manner of reasons for postponing forgiveness. One of these reasons is waiting for the wrongdoers to repent before we forgive them. Yet such a delay causes us to forfeit the peace and happiness that could be ours." – James E. Faust.

So, for you who haven't found faith, when the words "please forgive me" are not good enough and you need something tangible, what could that be?

I don't have an answer. Maybe a new car, a house, a new life? I think that forgiveness is something that is faith-driven. Not in a spiritual sense, even though it makes it easy to give and receive. Forgiveness isn't something you can physically touch or something that you can physically hand over. My whole life I have been told that Jesus died for my sins and I have already been forgiven. Being told and understanding is what it took for me, but in that part of my life I needed to see it. I know this defies belief but seeing it is what built my belief. This is where my faith-building started.

Enough of when, what, and why. How the hell do you do it?

To start, you have to be completely honest with yourself and then accept the consequences. No participation trophies here! No dumbing-down the action. And stop being liberal about what happened. Just accept it! Then look for the positives and learn from the negatives. And once you get to this stage, repeat, repeat, and repeat!

How did I forgive?

I am not the victim of my bad fortune; I am a strong woman who has overcome adversity! This is what I tell myself every day. I am who I need to become through all that I have experienced. It has never been easy, there are mornings I see the scars and flaws in my mirror, but I continue to remind myself there are mountains out there to conquer.

Any way you look at it, life is a journey filled with paths. Some easy, some hard, and some that look impossible. The beautiful part of our journey is that we get to choose which path to take. There is no judging which direction you take because there isn't anyone there to judge you, just you. Just remember to use your village.

I figure that I am halfway through my life and I have many things I would love to teach my children, my grandchildren, and the great staff that I work with every day. And through the mountains and valleys, I truly believe that I Get It Now, but I will never stop learning. My story isn't about becoming self-made; it's about finding my village.

Made in USA - Crawfordsville, IN
47152_9781734005509
04.01.2022 0621